T0146968

An Analysis of

Philip Zimbardo's

The Lucifer Effect
Understanding How
Good People Turn Evil

Alexander J. O'Connor

Published by Macat International Ltd
24:13 Coda Centre, 189 Munster Road, London SW6 6AW.

Distributed exclusively by Routledge
2 Park Square, Milton Park, Abingdon, Oxon OX14 4RN
711 Third Avenue, New York, NY 10017, USA

Routledge is an imprint of the Taylor & Francis Group, an informa business

www.macat.com
info@macat.com

Cataloguing in Publication Data
A catalogue record for this book is available from the British Library.
Library of Congress Cataloguing-in-Publication Data is available upon request.
Cover illustration: Etienne Gilfillan

ISBN 978-1-912303-69-4 (hardback)
ISBN 978-1-912128-55-6 (paperback)
ISBN 978-1-912282-57-9 (e-book)

Notice
The information in this book is designed to orientate readers of the work under analysis,
to elucidate and contextualise its key ideas and themes, and to aid in the development
of critical thinking skills. It is not meant to be used, nor should it be used, as a
substitute for original thinking or in place of original writing or research. References and
notes are provided for informational purposes and their presence does not constitute
endorsement of the information or opinions therein. This book is presented solely for
educational purposes. It is sold on the understanding that the publisher is not engaged
to provide any scholarly advice. The publisher has made every effort to ensure that
this book is accurate and up-to-date, but makes no warranties or representations with
regard to the completeness or reliability of the information it contains. The information
and the opinions provided herein are not guaranteed or warranted to produce particular
results and may not be suitable for students of every ability. The publisher shall not be
liable for any loss, damage or disruption arising from any errors or omissions, or from
the use of this book, including, but not limited to, special, incidental, consequential or
other damages caused, or alleged to have been caused, directly or indirectly, by the
information contained within.

CONTENTS

WAYS IN TO THE TEXT

Who Is Philip Zimbardo?   9
What Does *The Lucifer Effect* Say?   11
Why Does *The Lucifer Effect* Matter?   13

SECTION 1: INFLUENCES

Module 1: The Author and the Historical Context   16
Module 2: Academic Context   21
Module 3: The Problem   26
Module 4: The Author's Contribution   31

SECTION 2: IDEAS

Module 5: Main Ideas   37
Module 6: Secondary Ideas   42
Module 7: Achievement   48
Module 8: Place in the Author's Work   53

SECTION 3: IMPACT

Module 9: The First Responses   59
Module 10: The Evolving Debate   64
Module 11: Impact and Influence Today   69
Module 12: Where Next?   73

Glossary of Terms   78
People Mentioned in the Text   86
Works Cited   91

THE MACAT LIBRARY

The Macat Library is a series of unique academic explorations of seminal works in the humanities and social sciences – books and papers that have had a significant and widely recognised impact on their disciplines. It has been created to serve as much more than just a summary of what lies between the covers of a great book. It illuminates and explores the influences on, ideas of, and impact of that book. Our goal is to offer a learning resource that encourages critical thinking and fosters a better, deeper understanding of important ideas.

Each publication is divided into three Sections: Influences, Ideas, and Impact. Each Section has four Modules. These explore every important facet of the work, and the responses to it.

This Section-Module structure makes a Macat Library book easy to use, but it has another important feature. Because each Macat book is written to the same format, it is possible (and encouraged!) to cross-reference multiple Macat books along the same lines of inquiry or research. This allows the reader to open up interesting interdisciplinary pathways.

To further aid your reading, lists of glossary terms and people mentioned are included at the end of this book (these are indicated by an asterisk [*] throughout) – as well as a list of works cited.

Macat has worked with the University of Cambridge to identify the elements of critical thinking and understand the ways in which six different skills combine to enable effective thinking.
Three allow us to fully understand a problem; three more give us the tools to solve it. Together, these six skills make up the **PACIER** model of critical thinking. They are:

ANALYSIS – understanding how an argument is built
EVALUATION – exploring the strengths and weaknesses of an argument
INTERPRETATION – understanding issues of meaning

CREATIVE THINKING – coming up with new ideas and fresh connections
PROBLEM-SOLVING – producing strong solutions
REASONING – creating strong arguments

To find out more, visit **WWW.MACAT.COM.**

CRITICAL THINKING AND *THE LUCIFER EFFECT*

Primary critical thinking skill: PROBLEM-SOLVING
Secondary critical thinking skill: REASONING

What makes good people capable of committing bad – even evil – acts? Few psychologists are as well-qualified to answer that question as Philip Zimbardo, a psychology professor who was not only the author of the classic Stanford Prison Experiment – which asked two groups of students to assume the roles of prisoners and guards in a makeshift jail, to dramatic effect – but also an active participant in the trial of a US serviceman who took part in the violent abuse of Iraqi prisoners in the wake of the second Gulf War.

Zimbardo's book *The Lucifer Effect* is an extended analysis that aims to find solutions to the problem of how good people can commit evil acts. Zimbardo used his problem-solving skills to locate the solution to this question in an understanding of two conditions. Firstly, he writes, situational factors (circumstances and setting) must override dispositional ones, meaning that decent and well-meaning people can behave uncharacteristically when placed in unusual or stressful environments. Secondly, good and evil are not alternatives; they are interchangeable. Most people are capable of being both angels and devils, depending on the circumstances.

In making this observation, Zimbardo also built on the work of Stanley Milgram, whose own psychological experiments had shown the impact that authority figures can have on determining the actions of their subordinates. Zimbardo's book is a fine example of the importance of asking productive questions that go beyond the theoretical to consider real-world events.

ABOUT THE AUTHOR OF THE ORIGINAL WORK

Born in 1933, **Philip Zimbardo** is an American social psychologist and professor emeritus at Stanford University. His work on triggers of evil behaviour has made him famous yet controversial. In his 1971 Stanford Prison Experiment, he discovered that regular volunteers playing the role of guards in a mock prison quickly became abusive. Zimbardo later testified in defence of a US guard who committed acts of torture in Iraq's Abu Ghraib prison. His 2007 work, *The Lucifer Effect*, suggests it is more often 'bad barrels' rather than 'bad apples' that lead to such behaviour. Zimbardo has written many books investigating psychology and has received a number of prestigious awards. Now an anti-war and prison-reform activist, he continues to research topics including shyness and heroism, and promotes heroism in everyday life.

ABOUT THE AUTHOR OF THE ANALYSIS

Dr Alexander O'Connor did his postgraduate work at the University of California, Berkeley, where he received a PhD for work on social and personality psychology.

ABOUT MACAT

GREAT WORKS FOR CRITICAL THINKING

Macat is focused on making the ideas of the world's great thinkers accessible and comprehensible to everybody, everywhere, in ways that promote the development of enhanced critical thinking skills.

It works with leading academics from the world's top universities to produce new analyses that focus on the ideas and the impact of the most influential works ever written across a wide variety of academic disciplines. Each of the works that sit at the heart of its growing library is an enduring example of great thinking. But by setting them in context – and looking at the influences that shaped their authors, as well as the responses they provoked – Macat encourages readers to look at these classics and game-changers with fresh eyes. Readers learn to think, engage and challenge their ideas, rather than simply accepting them.

'Macat offers an amazing first-of-its-kind tool for interdisciplinary learning and research. Its focus on works that transformed their disciplines and its rigorous approach, drawing on the world's leading experts and educational institutions, opens up a world-class education to anyone.'

Andreas Schleicher
Director for Education and Skills, Organisation for Economic
Co-operation and Development

'Macat is taking on some of the major challenges in university education … They have drawn together a strong team of active academics who are producing teaching materials that are novel in the breadth of their approach.'

Prof Lord Broers,
former Vice-Chancellor of the University of Cambridge

'The Macat vision is exceptionally exciting. It focuses upon new modes of learning which analyse and explain seminal texts which have profoundly influenced world thinking and so social and economic development. It promotes the kind of critical thinking which is essential for any society and economy. This is the learning of the future.'

Rt Hon Charles Clarke, former UK Secretary of State for Education

'The Macat analyses provide immediate access to the critical conversation surrounding the books that have shaped their respective discipline, which will make them an invaluable resource to all of those, students and teachers, working in the field.'

Professor William Tronzo, University of California at San Diego

WAYS IN TO THE TEXT

KEY POINTS

- Born in 1933, Philip Zimbardo is an American social psychologist* and professor emeritus at Stanford University. Social psychology is the study of how people's social surroundings influence their thought processes, memories, learning, and behavior. He is known for his groundbreaking work on the effect that certain circumstances have on behavior.

- In *The Lucifer Effect* (2007), Zimbardo details the power of situations* (that is, aspects of a context that are external to the person serving as a focal point of analysis) to create evil. Evil here can refer to actions and people who intentionally cause physical, psychological, financial, or emotional harm and pain to others.

- Zimbardo uses his insights to detail in the book how and why some situations cause people to conform* to an idea of evil. Conforming is when individuals match their thought processes and behaviors to that of a wider group because of powerful social pressures.

Who Is Philip Zimbardo?

Philip Zimbardo, author of *The Lucifer Effect: Understanding How Good People Turn Evil* (2007), was born in 1933 in the South Bronx of New York City, an area he would later describe as "a ghetto" (a slum, usually occupied by a single minority community). Much of his childhood overlapped with the Great Depression* of 1929 to the late 1930s—an extreme economic recession causing profound financial hardship to much of the population of the United States. Zimbardo grew up poor.

In *The Lucifer Effect* (2007), Zimbardo describes how these circumstances affected his thinking and eventually his career, writing: "Urban ghetto life is all about surviving by developing useful 'street-smart' strategies. That means figuring out who has power that can be used against you or to help you, whom to avoid, and with whom you should ingratiate yourself."[1] Zimbardo explains that these experiences made him aware of the key roles held by power, and by particular situations, in affecting behavior and life outcomes.

His upbringing provoked his interest in psychology. In 1959, Zimbardo completed his PhD in psychology at Yale University, joining the psychology faculty at Stanford University in California in 1968, where he has remained ever since. Now professor emeritus at Stanford, Zimbardo remains active in both research and political activism.

In 2012, he wrote that since conducting a key piece of research, his "Stanford Prison Experiment" of 1971, he had "become a prison activist."[2] He has often advised and lectured policymakers and the judiciary on the negative psychological consequences of prison on prisoners. He is also founder of the Heroic Imagination Project (HIP),* a research body "dedicated to promoting heroism in everyday life."

Besides the Great Depression, two other major sociopolitical events shaped Zimbardo and his research. In the 1950s, many social psychologists began to study the topics of power, obedience, and evil in an attempt to explain the events and horrors that had occurred during World War II,* the global war of 1939–45 that began with Germany's invasion of Poland and ultimately involved many of the world's nations. This was also of interest to Zimbardo. Later, he opposed the United States' military involvement in the Vietnam War,* the 1955–75 armed conflict between communist North Vietnam and

South Vietnam, whose forces were supported by the US military after 1961. This opposition triggered his political and social activism.

What Does *The Lucifer Effect* Say?

In *The Lucifer Effect*, Zimbardo aims to provide psychological explanations of instances of evil.

Though he chooses not to explicitly define evil in the text, he relies on specific historical examples of "violence, anonymity, aggression, vandalism, torture, and terrorism"[3] to provide an implicit framework for what he considers to be evil. He specifically concentrates on the prison abuses perpetrated by members of the US military at Abu Ghraib prison* in Iraq, during the American-led invasion of that country in 2003.

In this case, American Army personnel tasked with guarding Iraqi detainees at Abu Ghraib prison repeatedly committed serious physical, psychological, and sexual abuse on the captives, often taking photographs to record the abuse. To many observers this was a surprising instance of sadistic* behavior (a sadist is a person who gets enjoyment from being violent or cruel, or causing pain to others). Zimbardo, however, claims that the abuse at Abu Ghraib should not be so surprising, as his 1971 Stanford Prison Experiment (SPE) demonstrated that ordinary people—even those who genuinely believed they would be incapable of harming others—are indeed capable of what Zimbardo calls "evil."

Zimbardo's core message in *The Lucifer Effect* is that situations can exert a great power over us. To illustrate this, he offers a detailed retelling and analysis of the SPE, a psychology study he designed and ran at Stanford University. The 24 participants were volunteers who agreed to live or work in a makeshift prison for two weeks. Zimbardo and his research assistants randomly assigned them to the role of either a prisoner or a guard, while he served as the prison superintendent. Under instruction to maintain order, the guards quickly began to abuse their roles, with Zimbardo observing as they psychologically and physically abused the prisoners. After just six days, the experiment had to be halted.

In *The Lucifer Effect,* published 26 years later, Zimbardo writes that the power of the overall situation and a host of situational factors were responsible for the transformation of the guards. He states that the SPE "emerged as a powerful illustration of the potentially toxic impact of bad systems and bad situations in making good people behave in pathological ways that are alien to their nature."[4]

In the book, Zimbardo uses his detailed findings from the SPE, along with other supporting studies accumulated since, to analyze other instances of sadistic, shocking, and evil events that have occurred throughout history, focusing on the prison abuses at Abu Ghraib.

Zimbardo becomes part of the story, just as he was in the SPE. He served as expert witness in the trial of one of the guards, Ivan Frederick,* who was eventually convicted of the assault and maltreatment of detainees at Abu Ghraib. The social psychologist Robert Levine* wrote in his review of the book: "By the time Zimbardo has finished describing Frederick's transformation from idealistic soldier to abuser, Abu Ghraib feels eerily indistinguishable from the Stanford Prison Experiment. It is as if the Iraqi prison had been designed by twisted social psychologists who wanted to replicate Zimbardo's experiment using real guards and prisoners."[5]

Finally, Zimbardo discusses how systemic factors* (that is, the influence of large-scale systems such as governments, cultures, economies, and organizations) tend to set up the bad conditions that allow for the bad situations that, in turn, elicit evil behavior. He concludes the text with a study on how people can avoid these bad situations and resist situational forces* to behave badly, much as he claims someone acting heroically would. Such situational forces are psychological pressures that are placed on a person by the circumstances surrounding them, whether they are aware of these pressures or not.

Why Does *The Lucifer Effect* Matter?

While *The Lucifer Effect* includes a wealth of information on social psychology, research ethics, and many historical events, it is mainly important because of its in-depth investigation of Zimbardo's own Stanford Prison Experiment—now recognized as a seminal study in the field of psychology. In examining the experiment, Zimbardo describes the social and psychological factors he believes are largely responsible for the outcome of the SPE (along with other evils such as the abuse at Abu Ghraib prison). He also analyses the Enron* scandal (an instance of widespread institutional corruption and fraud discovered at the US energy company Enron Corporation in 2001), the Rwanda genocides* (where up to one million people, mostly from the Tutsi ethnic minority, were slaughtered in 1994, primarily by Rwanda's Hutu majority), and the Roman Catholic Church sexual-abuse scandals* (the multiple cases of sexual abuse committed by Catholic clergymen worldwide in recent decades).

Yet Zimbardo offers hope and advice for readers of *The Lucifer Effect* so they can better understand instances of "evil" behavior: "I have proposed that we give greater consideration and more weight to situational and systemic processes than we typically do when we are trying to account for aberrant behaviors and seeming personality changes. Human behavior is always subject to situational forces."[6]

Most of all, Zimbardo hopes that a better knowledge of these treacherous situational forces allow people, in their own lives, to detect and resist the powerful pressure to act badly in certain situations: "In all the research cited and in our real-world examples, there were always some individuals who resisted [situational influences and evil], who did not yield to temptation. What delivered them from evil was not some inherent magical goodness but rather, more likely, an understanding, however intuitive, of mental and social tactics of resistance."[7]

For Zimbardo, heroism, like evil, is not something people are born with, but something his readers, and anyone, can learn to develop.

Finally, *The Lucifer Effect* offers Zimbardo's insights into some of the controversies stimulated by the Stanford Prison Experiment and also his wider ideas. Referencing those controversies throughout the book, Zimbardo provides both analytical and historical background into one of the key criticisms of the experiment: that it was an unethical study. Zimbardo dedicates a chapter specifically to research ethics and the SPE, discussing his beliefs on the experiment's ethics and his own ethical failings.

NOTES

1   Philip Zimbardo, *The Lucifer Effect: Understanding How Good People Turn Evil* (New York: Random House, 2007), xi.

2   Scott Drury, Scott A. Hutchens, Duane E. Shuttlesworth, and Carole L. White, "Philip G. Zimbardo on His Career and the Stanford Prison Experiment's 40th Anniversary," *History of Psychology* 15, no. 2 (2012): 162.

3   Zimbardo, *Lucifer*, xi.

4   Zimbardo, *Lucifer*, 195.

5   Robert Levine, "The Evil That Men Do," *American Scientist*, September–October 2007, accessed September 15, 2015, http://www.americanscientist.org/bookshelf/content2/2007/5/the-evil-that-men-do.

6   Zimbardo, *Lucifer*, 445.

7   Zimbardo, *Lucifer*, xiii.

SECTION 1
INFLUENCES

MODULE 1
THE AUTHOR AND THE
HISTORICAL CONTEXT

KEY POINTS

- *The Lucifer Effect* is the most extensive analysis of Philip Zimbardo's famed 1971 Stanford Prison Experiment (SPE).* This study had gained renewed significance as Zimbardo has applied his findings from the SPE to offer insights into more recent—and real—acts of evil.

- As a student, Zimbardo worked in New York City's theater district. He developed an appreciation for, and understanding of, drama and production values (the details and finesse that contribute to a successful theatrical experience) that were later apparent in his design of the SPE.

- Several historical events pushed Zimbardo toward a career in social psychology* (the study of how thought and behavior are influenced by social surroundings) and political and social activism. They were, in particular, the Great Depression,* an economic downturn that began in 1929, and the Vietnam War,* a conflict in which the United States fought between 1961–75 with the loss of many lives.

Why Read This Text?

Philip Zimbardo's *The Lucifer Effect: Understanding How Good People Turn Evil* (2007) provides an account of some of the situational* factors (that is, the external factors such as context, surroundings, and so on, that affect the person being studied) that lead ordinary people to commit unethical, deviant, destructive, and "evil" behavior. In a review

> ❝ I guess you could say I was an intuitive psychologist and 'situationist'* from the beginning. I was born at home, hands first, in New York City's South Bronx ghetto during the Great Depression, and we moved 31 times while I was a child. ❞
>
> Philip Zimbardo, *On 50 Years of Giving Psychology Away: An Interview With Philip Zimbardo*

of *The Lucifer Effect*, the political scientist Rose McDermott* wrote, "This remarkable and riveting new book by the creator of the classic Stanford Prison Experiment (SPE) deserves to be required reading for all those interested in the intersection of psychological processes and political reality."[1]

Zimbardo draws the majority of the text's empirical evidence (that is, its evidence verifiable by observation) from his famed SPE study, conducted in 1971. That study showed how quickly ordinary people could behave in "evil" ways when placed in particular circumstances. It remains one of the most well-known, dramatic, and important experiments in social psychology.* As the social psychologist Robert Levine* writes: "The Stanford Prison Experiment has become a cornerstone of social psychology … What happened at Stanford makes it clear that insane situations can create insane behavior even in normal people."[2]

The SPE has also become one of the most reviewed and analyzed studies in the field. Yet in *The Lucifer Effect*, Zimbardo gives new life to the already seminal SPE study. He combines original and new interpretations of the experiment and introduces more recent research, as he offers explanations for many evils that have occurred in the world since the 1970s. Zimbardo provides the most extensive written account of the experiment to date—including a dramatic retelling of the entire procedure, transcripts of the study, and interviews with participants.

Zimbardo also introduces in the book a new understanding of the SPE. He explains that he has come to view systemic factors* (that is, the influence of large-scale organizations or systems) as responsible for many of the situations that elicit evil. Therefore, he sees systemic factors as worthy of examination by psychologists.

Author's Life

Zimbardo was born in 1933 in the urban ghettos—deprived neighborhoods—of New York City, growing up poor in the years of the Great Depression. As a child he endured a lengthy hospitalization for respiratory illness, and while he was treated in isolation, he saw many sick children die around him. Zimbardo later recalled that the "experience of extreme isolation at a very formative time in my childhood really gave me a push in the direction of not only being a social psychologist, but of wanting to study things and do things that improve the quality of human life."[3]

His childhood experiences of urban poverty, and of ingratiating himself with the neighborhood gangs, were also influential. Zimbardo recalled that he and his friends "had initiation rituals that each new kid had to go through to gain admission to the gang, a series of daring deeds that had to be accomplished in one day."[4] The psychology behind such initiations became a theme of his later work, including the SPE. Zimbardo wanted to examine the willingness of ordinary people to forego their own moral standards and normal behavior simply to gain acceptance into a group.

As a teenage student, Zimbardo worked at a theater in New York's Broadway District. He later recalled that this "taught me about the virtues of performing really well"[5]—virtues that became apparent later in his elaborate production and staging of the SPE.

Zimbardo went on to complete his PhD in psychology at Yale University in 1959. In 1968, he became professor of psychology at Stanford University. Now professor emeritus at the university,

Zimbardo continues to research new fields, including shyness, heroism, terrorism, and the perception of time. He is founder of the Heroic Imagination Project (HIP),* a research body dedicated to promoting heroic behavior in everyday life.

Author's Background

By his own admission, Zimbardo was shaped by three major sociopolitical events that occurred during his childhood and early career—the Great Depression, World War II,* and the Vietnam War. Foremost, Zimbardo grew up poor, like many others in America during the Great Depression. He later recalled the pain of feeling judged, and even perceived as less than human, due to his family's financial plight. In one interview, Zimbardo said that "being hurt personally triggered a curiosity about how such beliefs are formed, how attitudes can influence people's behavior, how people can feel so strongly about something they know nothing about."[6]

America's military involvement in Vietnam in the 1960s and 1970s, also influenced Zimbardo; he describes it as the trigger for his later political and social activism. A prominent anti-war campaigner, he has also demanded changes to the American prison system. In a 2012 interview, Zimbardo said, "I have too much to say, and I now have a reputation that I can use for certain causes like being against war, being a peace activist, and now, trying to create everyday heroes."[7]

NOTES

1 Rose McDermott, "Reviewed Work: *The Lucifer Effect: Understanding How Good People Turn Evil* by Philip Zimbardo," *Political Psychology* 28, No. 5 (2007): 644.

2 Robert Levine, "The Evil That Men Do," *American Scientist,* September–October 2007, accessed September 15, 2015, http://www.americanscientist.org/bookshelf/content2/2007/5/the-evil-that-men-do.

3   Christina Maslach, "Emperor of the Edge," *Psychology Today*, September 1,
    2000, accessed September 15, 2015, https://www.psychologytoday.com/
    articles/200009/emperor-the-edge.

4   Philip Zimbardo, "Recollections of a Social Psychologist's Career: An
    Interview with Dr. Philip Zimbardo," *Journal of Social Behavior and
    Personality* 14, No. 1 (1999): 2.

5   George M. Slavich, "On 50 Years of Giving Psychology Away: An Interview
    with Philip Zimbardo," *Teaching of Psychology* 36, no. 4 (2009): 280.

6   Maslach, "Emperor of the Edge," *Psychology Today*.

7   Scott Drury, Scott A. Hutchens, Duane E. Shuttlesworth, and Carole L. White,
    "Philip G. Zimbardo on His Career and the Stanford Prison Experiment's 40th
    Anniversary," *History of Psychology* 15, no. 2 (2012): 164.

ACADEMIC CONTEXT

KEY POINTS

- In the 1960s and 1970s, there was an ongoing debate between social psychologists* (those who study how people's mental processes and behaviors are influenced by their social surroundings) and personality psychologists* (those who study individual differences in people's mental processes and behaviors). Each group argued for the relative influence of situational factors versus personality factors on a person's behavior.

- Social psychologists Muzafer Sherif* and Solomon Asch* have provided some of the strongest evidence of the power of situations* to determine behavior.

- Yale University psychology professor Stanley Milgram,* whose work particularly influenced Philip Zimbardo, provided even more dramatic evidence of the power of situations.

The Work in its Context

Although Philip Zimbardo's *The Lucifer Effect: Understanding How Good People Turn Evil* was published in 2007, it is largely a retelling of the 1971 Stanford Prison Experiment (SPE).* As a result, the book is a product of two eras.

In the early 1970s, psychology was in the midst of what people called the cognitive revolution.* This began in the 1950s and affected a number of academic fields including psychology, anthropology, and linguistics.

The cognitive revolution was broadly a move away from behaviorism,* which concentrated on studying observable behaviors,

> ❝ Beginning in the 1950s, attention in social psychology started to turn toward the powerful and sometimes counterintuitive effects that social situations could have on how people think, feel, and behave. ❞
>
> Ludy T. Benjamin Jr.* and Jeffry A. Simpson,* *The Power of the Situation*

replacing it with a focus on the study of a person's cognitions*—that is, the inner workings of the mind, thoughts, attitudes, motivations, mental abilities, memories, and values that make up a person's inner life.

Zimbardo's specific field was social psychology (the study of how people's social surroundings influence their cognitions and behaviors). Social psychology and its partner field, personality psychology* (the study of individual differences in people's thought processes and behaviors), were also in debate over the primary influence of behavior. Was it the person and his or her internal attitudes—what psychologists call dispositions*—that determined behavior? Or did the power of situations outweigh individual personalities?

Walter Mischel,* professor of psychology at Columbia University, is often credited as sparking this so-called "person-situation debate."* Mischel described the debate as being about the consistency "with which the same person reacts to situations that ostensibly are relatively similar (that is, selected to evoke the same trait), and most important, the utility of predictions based on global trait inferences."[1] In the field of personality psychology, a "trait" refers to a disposition, or a somewhat consistent pattern of behavior or cognition. Mischel questioned whether these traits can reliably and meaningfully predict behavior.

Mischel argued the importance of considering dispositions, situations, *and* the interaction between them—an approach described as "interactionist."* However, other psychologists focused their research on just one factor. At that time, Zimbardo concentrated on situations as the prime determinant of behavior.

By the time *The Lucifer Effect* was published in 2007, most psychologists had accepted that dispositional factors (internal characteristics such as personality traits) and situational factors (the conscious or unconscious psychological pressures placed on a person by the situation around them), and their interactions were all integral for predicting and explaining behavior. A more recent research movement, named positive psychology,* had also become relevant by that time. Proponents of positive psychology seek to change the questions that psychologists traditionally ask—away from a focus on negative outcomes, such as how and why people become depressed, and towards a focus on positive outcomes, such as how and why people thrive.

Overview of the Field

By the mid-1950s, a number of social psychologists were already successfully proving the power with which situational factors can determine human behavior. An early and clear example was the 1954 Robber's Cave Experiment* conducted by the social psychologists Muzafer Sherif* and Carolyn Sherif.* At a summer camp in Oklahoma in the United States, they randomly divided 22 young boys into two groups and then placed them in a series of manipulated situations. As a result, the boys' attitudes and behaviors changed. After competitive games, hostility and stereotyping increased between groups. Meanwhile, after cooperative tasks, hostility and stereotyping decreased.

Around the same time, the social psychologist Solomon Asch ran a series of studies on conformity* (when individuals match their thoughts and behaviors to that of a wider group, due to social pressures) that highlighted the power of situations to dictate behavior, often in unexpected ways. In his most well-known task, he presented study participants with a straight black line and then asked them to choose which one matched the original from a set of straight black lines of varying lengths. Unbeknownst to the participant, he or she was not surrounded by fellow participants. Rather, Asch had paid everyone else in the group and instructed them to give a (matching) incorrect response purposely.

This study clearly illustrated the power of the situation and of a majority group. Although it was obvious which of the lines did match in length, participants often publically submitted the incorrect answer, conforming to the answer that the majority of the group provided. Asch reported: "A substantial proportion of subjects yielded once their confidence was shaken. The presumed rightness of the majority deprived them of the resolution to report their own observations."[2] The Sherif and Asch studies demonstrate how situational pressures, such as the formation of groups and a person's subsequent conformity to that group, can cause people to behave unexpectedly.

Academic Influences

In his work on the Stanford Prison Experiment, and on the causes of evil and heroism, Zimbardo was following in the footsteps of Sherif and Asch as he argued that situations and group pressures have enormous influence. However, the psychologist Stanley Milgram, who was also Zimbardo's friend and former high school classmate, was the person who most directly influenced him. Zimbardo later recalled that even in high school, Milgram had been fascinated by the power of situations: "Milgram was concerned about the Holocaust even back then … His work on blind obedience to authority really derived from his concern about whether the same thing could happen here [in the US]."[3] "The Holocaust" refers to the genocide, orchestrated by Nazi Germany and its leader Adolf Hitler, of about six million European Jews and other ethnic and social minorities during World War II.*

In the early 1960s, Milgram, then psychology professor at Yale University, ran a groundbreaking "obedience to authority"* study. He instructed volunteers to give electric shocks to a stranger, allegedly for an experiment on learning. Unaware that the shocks were not real, most participants administered increasingly powerful and seemingly painful and dangerous shocks, despite their own fear and distress at doing so, simply because an experimenter instructed them to continue. Many people progressed to a level that would have been lethal if real.

Milgram's colleagues and the public were surprised by the results of the highly controversial study, which was the most dramatic illustration at the time of the power of the situation (and people's innate obedience to authorities) on behaviors. Zimbardo later argued that "[Milgram] was really the first person to say that it's not enough to think or say that you won't do something. Indeed, it's not even enough to imagine you're in a situation, because it's something about being in powerful social settings that is transformative."[4]

NOTES

1   Walter Mischel, "Toward a Cognitive Social Learning Reconceptualization of Personality," *Psychological Review* 80, no. 4 (1973): 255.

2   Solomon E. Asch, "Studies of Independence and Conformity: I. A Minority of One Against a Unanimous Majority," *Psychological Monographs: General and Applied* 70, no. 9 (1956): 70.

3   George M. Slavich, "On 50 Years of Giving Psychology Away: An Interview with Philip Zimbardo." *Teaching of Psychology* 36, no. 4 (2009): 279.

4   Slavich, "Giving," 279.

MODULE 3
THE PROBLEM

KEY POINTS

- In 2003, during the United States' invasion of Iraq, American military personnel working at Abu Ghraib* prison in Baghdad committed physical abuse, sexual assaults, and torture on Iraqi detainees. There were also claims that American psychologists were complicit in the abuse.

- Many social psychologists* and independent investigators argued that situational factors* were largely to blame for the abuse at Abu Ghraib.

- Philip Zimbardo, referencing his Stanford Prison Experiment (SPE),* became an expert witness in the trial of one of the Abu Ghraib guards and was outspoken about the likely role of situational factors.

Core Question

Philip Zimbardo's *The Lucifer Effect: Understanding How Good People Turn Evil* (2007) seeks to examine and explain the prisoner abuses committed at Abu Ghraib prison in Baghdad in 2003. US military prison guards there carried out a sustained campaign of psychological and physical torture and sexual abuse of detainees, with many instances recorded on camera.

Zimbardo was already considered a leading expert on prison mentality and sadistic* behavior (that is, finding pleasure in causing suffering to others.) He entered the debate on Abu Ghraib in 2004, writing an opinion piece for the *Boston Globe* that stated, "Unless we learn the dynamics of 'why,' we will never be able to counteract the powerful forces that can transform ordinary people into evil perpetrators."[1] In this way, Zimbardo urged both researchers and the

> ❝ The horrifying photos of young Iraqis abused by American soldiers have shocked the world with their depictions of human degradation, forcing us to acknowledge that some of our beloved soldiers have committed barbarous acts of cruelty and sadism. ❞
>
> Philip Zimbardo, *Power Turns Good Soldiers into "Bad Apples."*

public to consider the importance of situational causes in the Abu Ghraib case.

Soon after the abuse at Abu Ghraib came to the public's attention, some news reports claimed that American psychologists were also involved in the administration of torture techniques on detainees captured in Iraq. Additional reports soon implicated the American Psychological Association (APA),* the scientific and professional organization that represents psychologists in the United States. These reports claimed the APA was assisting the American government in its search for effective interrogation techniques. People began to question whether such techniques amounted to torture—especially as the APA had expressly forbidden its members from supporting torture.

In 2006, the APA's committee on ethics and national security reiterated its previous stance, declaring that "there are no exceptional circumstances whatsoever … that may be invoked as a justification for torture, including the invocation of laws, regulations or orders."[2] Nonetheless, various sources and reports continued to accuse APA members and leaders of either supporting or administering torture tactics. By drawing on his experiences from the Stanford Prison Experiment (SPE), Zimbardo was uniquely placed to address the abuses at Abu Ghraib, the American government's use of torture, and the role of psychologists in both of those contentious situations.

The Participants

Most social psychologists, when writing about the abuse at Abu Ghraib and the acceptance of torture by military officials and psychologists, tended to rely on situational explanations, arguing that the perpetrators had been affected by various psychological pressures created by the wider situations around them.

To support their accounts, these scholars often referenced the psychologist Stanley Milgram's* obedience studies (in which volunteers had been prepared to administer powerful electric shocks to strangers on the orders of an authority figure) and Philip Zimbardo's SPE (where ordinary people had rapidly become abusive of other volunteers who were under their control).

The social psychologist Susan T. Fiske* called Milgram's and Zimbardo's work "illuminating" in relation to the case of Abu Ghraib, writing: "Guards abuse prisoners in conformity* with what other guards do, in order to fulfill a potent role; this is illustrated by the Stanford Prison study."[3] Fiske argues, too, that these findings would be of benefit if considered when official policies were being formed: "Society holds individuals responsible for their actions, as the military court-martial* recognizes, but social psychology suggests we should also hold responsible peers and superiors who control the social context."[4]

In 2004, the US Department of Defense (DoD), the branch of government charged with military matters, commissioned an independent panel to investigate the Abu Ghraib abuse case. The panel's findings also allocated blame to both situational factors and the higher authorities involved in the prison, as well as the wider US military. The committee presented its findings in the Schlesinger report,* an independent investigation into the Abu Ghraib prison abuse led by James Schlesinger in 2004, noting: "The abuses were not just the failure of some individuals to follow known standards, and they are more than the failure of a few leaders to enforce proper discipline."[5] The committee continued: "There is both institutional and personal responsibility at higher levels."[6]

The Contemporary Debate

Using both academic channels and the press, Zimbardo spoke publicly about the similarities between the events and abuses at Abu Ghraib and those that occurred during his Stanford Prison Experiment (SPE). Using his findings from the SPE, Zimbardo argued that situational and systemic factors were primarily at fault for the abuses at the Iraqi prison. In 2004, he wrote an opinion piece in the *Boston Globe*, saying that he considered the American soldiers involved in the abuse were probably "once-good apples, soured and corrupted by an evil barrel."[7] He also referred to the psychologist Stanley Milgram's obedience studies to reinforce this point.

Soon afterwards, in late 2004, Zimbardo participated in the legal defense of Ivan Frederick,* a staff sergeant in the US Army being court-martialed (prosecuted in a military court) for his role in the abuse and torture of detainees at Abu Ghraib. Acting for the defense team, Zimbardo and other psychologists and medical professionals assessed Frederick's psychological history. Zimbardo later served as an expert witness at the trial.

Writing in *The Lucifer Effect,* Zimbardo recalls his testimony and how he "outlined … some parallels between the Stanford Prison Experiment and the environment of abuse at Abu Ghraib Prison."[8] He also "argued that the situation had brought out the aberrant behaviors in which [Frederick] engaged and for which he is both sorry and guilty."[9]

Social psychologists and the military all seemed to agree that situational factors were evident in the Abu Ghraib abuses. However, Zimbardo was not convinced that the court-martial received the message, and he was displeased with Frederick's sentence, which included eight years in a military prison. Zimbardo believed the US government and military wished to adopt and promote the idea that these were a "few rogue soldiers, the 'bad apples' in the otherwise good US Army barrel."[10]

NOTES

1   Philip G. Zimbardo, "Power turns good soldiers into 'bad apples,'" *The Boston Globe*, May 9, 2004, accessed September 16, 2015, http://www. boston.com/news/globe/editorial_opinion/oped/articles/2004/05/09/ power_turns_good_soldiers_into_bad_apples/.

2   Olivia Moorehead-Slaughter, "Ethics and National Security," *Monitor on Psychology*, April 2006, accessed September 17, 2015, http://www.apa. org/monitor/apr06/security.aspx.

3   Susan T. Fiske, L. T. Harris, and A. J. Cuddy. "Social Psychology. Why Ordinary People Torture Enemy Prisoners." *Science* 306, no. 5701 (2004): 1482–3.

4   Fiske et al., *Ordinary*, 1482.

5   John H. Cushman, Jr., "Outside Panel Faults Leaders of Pentagon for Prisoner Abuse," *New York Times*, August 24, 2004, accessed September 17, 2015, http://www.nytimes.com/2004/08/24/politics/24CND-ABUS.html.

6   Cushman, Jr., "Outside Panel Faults Leaders of Pentagon for Prisoner Abuse".

7   Zimbardo, "Power turns good soldiers into 'bad apples.'"

8   Philip Zimbardo, *The Lucifer Effect: Understanding How Good People Turn Evil* (New York: Random House, 2007), 370.

9   Zimbardo, *Lucifer*, 370.

10 Zimbardo, *Lucifer*, 371.

THE AUTHOR'S CONTRIBUTION

KEY POINTS

- In *The Lucifer Effect*, Philip Zimbardo aims to illustrate the power of situations,* relying primarily on evidence from his 1971 Stanford Prison Experiment (SPE)* and the prison abuses at Abu Ghraib.*

- Zimbardo had unprecedented access to the data from both the SPE and Abu Ghraib, allowing him to make comparisons that others could not.

- Susan T. Fiske* and other social psychologists also promoted the "situationist"* school of thought, which argues that situations are often responsible for eliciting evil behaviors from ordinary people.

Author's Aims

In *The Lucifer Effect* Philip Zimbardo aims to provide both evidence and theory on when, how, and why certain situations can lead ordinary people to surprisingly sadistic* and evil behaviors. This was aimed at not only academics in his field but also the general public.

To prove his theories, Zimbardo provides an extensive account of his 1971 Stanford Prison Experiment (SPE). He then uses more recent historical examples, particularly the abuses that occurred at Abu Ghraib during the US invasion of Iraq of 2003, to support his evidence. These were particularly relatable to the SPE. Both events took place in a prison setting and, in both cases, the guards showed unexpectedly sadistic behaviors by insulting, depriving of sleep, and psychologically manipulating prisoners—although the Abu Ghraib guards also committed much more heinous acts of sexual abuse and physical torture.

> **❝** The parallels between the abuses at Abu Ghraib and the events in the SPE have given our Stanford prison experience added validity, which in turn sheds light on the psychological dynamics that contributed to creating horrific abuses in that real prison. **❞**
>
> Philip Zimbardo, *The Lucifer Effect: Understanding How Good People Turn Evil*

In the book, Zimbardo expands his arguments beyond the situational factors that he had described and promoted in the years since the SPE. He writes of *The Lucifer Effect*, "Had I written this book shortly after the end of the Stanford Prison Experiment, I would have been content to detail the ways in which situational forces are more powerful than we think … [but] I would have missed the big picture, the bigger power for creating evil out of good—that of the System."[1]

In *The Lucifer Effect,* Zimbardo casts his attention one level up, toward the large-scale systems, such as governments, cultures, or organizations that enable the dangerous situations that, in turn, provoke and elicit evil.

Zimbardo's final major aim in the book is to examine, and share, how people can avoid the situational and systemic* factors that might push them towards bad behavior. Following early reports of the Abu Ghraib abuses, the psychologist Susan F. Fiske and her coauthors challenged the field of social psychology to better understand when and why people do *not* succumb to situational pressures. Fiske wrote in *Science* in 2004 that "explaining evils such as Abu Ghraib demonstrates scientific principles that could help to avert them."[2] Zimbardo heeded this call, and devotes some space in *The Lucifer Effect* to providing prescriptions for how best to avoid the situational forces* that tend to elicit abusive behaviors.

Approach

To demonstrate how powerful situations can lead ordinary people to harm others, Zimbardo relies on the data of the Stanford Prison Experiment. In *The Lucifer Effect*, he is able to provide an exhaustive account of the SPE, including detailed and previously unpublished transcripts and descriptions of video footage of the experiment.

Zimbardo was given privileged and unfettered access to information while acting as an expert witness at the court martial* (military trial) of former staff sergeant Ivan Frederick* for his actions at Abu Ghraib. Zimbardo describes in *The Lucifer Effect* how he received comprehensive access to the case. "I became more like an investigative reporter than a social psychologist,"[3] he writes. "I worked at uncovering everything I could about this young man, from intensive interviews with him and conversations and correspondence with [those who knew him] … I was given access to all of the many hundreds of digitally documented images of depravity … [and] was provided with all of the then available reports from various military and civilian investigating committees."[4] Following these experiences, Zimbardo is able to provide an unprecedented account of how situational factors—many of which are present in most prisons—can enable some of the abuses and torture that occurred both in the SPE and at Abu Ghraib.

Those two situations were comparable due to their prison dynamic. However, Zimbardo discusses other real instances where situations have elicited evil actions in the decades since the SPE. These cases range from the corporate fraud committed at the US energy company Enron* to the 1994 genocides in Rwanda,* in which a million people from the Tutsi minority ethnic group were slaughtered, to the widespread sexual abuse committed by priests in the Roman Catholic Church.* In those varied instances, Zimbardo is able to demonstrate how many of the same situational explanations and group pressures helped to make these events possible. These include the need to belong to social groups (social psychologists believe the desire to be accepted by others is a fundamental human need), and the pressure to conform once in a group (by altering one's thought processes and behaviors to match those shared by the wider group).

Contribution in Context

Since the 1960s, Philip Zimbardo, Stanley Milgram,* and other psychologists had been proponents of the power of the situation—the ability of situational factors to influence behavior, often overriding the influence of dispositional* factors like innate personality traits. This "situationist" school of thought was widely accepted, particularly as an explanation for the behavior of people placed in novel and stressful situations.

For many of the prison guards at Abu Ghraib, both conditions were true—they were newly stationed as prison guards and then forced to quell numerous prisoner riots, while also facing the threat of outside forces invading the prison. In 2004, Fiske and her coauthors wrote: "Virtually anyone can be aggressive if sufficiently provoked, stressed, disgruntled, or hot. The situation of the 800th Military Police Brigade guarding Abu Ghraib prisoners fit all the social conditions known to cause aggression."[5]

This school of thought was largely based on the seminal work that Milgram and Zimbardo carried out in the 1960s and 1970s. To a degree, in *The Lucifer Effect* Zimbardo is largely revisiting his own established ideology for a modern audience, as well as updating his ideas with the benefit of decades of additional evidence.

NOTES

1   Philip Zimbardo, *The Lucifer Effect: Understanding How Good People Turn Evil* (New York: Random House, 2007), x.

2   Susan T. Fiske, L. T. Harris, and A. J. Cuddy. "Social Psychology. Why Ordinary People Torture Enemy Prisoners." *Science* 306, no. 5701 (2004): 1483.

3   Zimbardo, *Lucifer*, ix.

4   Zimbardo, *Lucifer*, ix–x.

5   Fiske, et al. "Ordinary:" 1483.

SECTION 2
IDEAS

MODULE 5
MAIN IDEAS

KEY POINTS

- In *The Lucifer Effect*, Philip Zimbardo argues that nearly everyone is capable of unethical and evil behavior when under pressure from certain situational* or systemic* factors.

- The Stanford Prison Experiment (SPE) proves the ability of seemingly normal people to act sadistically*—that is, to derive pleasure from cruel behavior—and Zimbardo suggests that similar situational and systemic factors existed at the Abu Ghraib* prison.

- In the book, Zimbardo uses metaphors to summarize his themes and provides a dramatic and detailed retelling of the SPE, which conveys the extent to which ordinary people can transform into evil.

Key Themes

In *The Lucifer Effect*, Philip Zimbardo examines the influence of external forces in "pushing us toward engaging in deviant, destructive, or evil behavior."[1] He does not define or restrict the evil behaviors that, he argues, are enabled by external forces. In fact, he does not define in the text what he considers the word "evil" to mean, despite the concept's key role. Instead, he relies on providing examples of such behaviors, concentrating on the abuses that occurred during the SPE and at Abu Ghraib prison.

Zimbardo's analysis has two key themes running through it:
- First, that good and evil are permeable (meaning, in this instance, interchangeable). Zimbardo suggests that "it is possible for angels to become devils and … for devils to become angels."[2] Therefore most people are capable of both.

> ❝ One of the dominant conclusions of the Stanford Prison Experiment is that the pervasive yet subtle power of a host of situational variables can dominate an individual's will to resist. ❞
>
> Philip Zimbardo, *The Lucifer Effect: Understanding How Good People Turn Evil*

- Second, that external forces are more responsible than dispositional factors* (that is, an individual's own personality) for much of the world's evil. Zimbardo suggests that a hierarchy of influence exists, with systemic factors (such as governments, organizations or cultures) being the most effective conductors of evil, then situational forces, and finally dispositions.

As he considers the second of these themes, Zimbardo revises the idiom of "a few bad apples." This traditional phrase states that every barrel of apples contains at least a few bad ones—and it is intended as a metaphor, implying that every group of people will contain a few bad people. The fact that this metaphor exists, according to Zimbardo, is evidence of people's tendency to assume that the primary cause of evil behavior is the individual's innate disposition. But he says, "The *bad apple-dispositional* view ignores the apple barrel and its potentially corrupting situational impact on those within it."[3]

Zimbardo prefers an analysis that focuses "on the barrel makers, on those with the power to design the barrel."[4] In place of the traditional idiom, he suggests a more reflective metaphor of bad barrels, rather than bad apples. Zimbardo writes that "barrel makers" can include nearly anyone with the power to shape situations and direct behavior: governments, corporate leaders, sports coaches, military leaders, religious leaders, and even Zimbardo himself, as lead experimenter in the SPE.

Exploring the Ideas

Many of the ideas and evidence behind Zimbardo's key themes come from the SPE. In this 1971 study, Zimbardo created a makeshift prison in the basement of Stanford University's psychology department and randomly assigned 24 young male volunteers the role of either prisoner or guard. Zimbardo, who played the role of prison superintendent, writes that randomly assigning participants to the role of guard "ensured that they were initially good apples and were corrupted by the insidious power of the bad barrel, this prison."[5]

In other words, both the prisoners and guards could have been considered interchangeable before the start of the study. Assuming power, based only on the randomness of their assignment to the role, the guards soon verbally abused prisoners, forced them into physical labor, intentionally disrupted their sleep, and secluded some into solitary confinement.*

The experiment was scheduled to last two weeks, but Zimbardo canceled it at the end of the first week after several prisoners became anguished at the physical and psychological abuse that the guards inflicted on them. Zimbardo recaps the effect that this abuse had on the prisoners, writing in *The Lucifer Effect*: "Half of our student prisoners had to be released early because of severe emotional and cognitive disorders."[6]

Zimbardo then applies his analysis to the prison abuse and torture that occurred at Abu Ghraib and claims that they parallel those found during the SPE, being only more atrocious in scale. Both instances were made possible, Zimbardo claims, because of situational and systemic factors.

Zimbardo describes many similar situational factors in both settings. He states that "boredom operated in both settings,"[7] that the guards were not properly trained, and that they had total power with little accountability. In relation to the wider systemic factors, Zimbardo argues that a "culture of abuse"[8] existed during the Iraq War, facilitated by the US government and military command. He writes that they employed "torture tactics—under sanitized terms—and failed to provide the leadership, oversight, accountability, and mission-specific training necessary."[9] US government officials, for instance, framed the invasion of Iraq as part of their "war on terror"[10] and used the term "enhanced interrogation" rather than torture. From Zimbardo's perspective, such policies probably helped to normalize and justify the abuse of Iraqi prisoners.

Language and Expression

As labels for some of his main themes, Zimbardo used metaphors and idioms. The most prominent example of this is his reformulation of the bad apple metaphor to introduce the idea of bad barrels. Another is the title, *The Lucifer Effect,* which references the story of Lucifer* from Christian mythology. Lucifer was an angel of God who epitomized everything good and moral—before he fell from God's grace and transformed into the most evil of beings. Zimbardo asks his readers, "Could we, like God's favorite angel, Lucifer, ever be led into the temptation to do the unthinkable to others?"[11] Zimbardo's answer is a clear "yes," and the story of Lucifer serves as an apt example of this moral transformation. Although they are simplifications, the bad apple and Lucifer metaphors are useful entry points, and summaries, of Zimbardo's key themes.

Zimbardo devotes much of the text to the description of his 1971 Stanford Prison Experiment (SPE). He characterizes that as a "chapter-by-chapter chronology … presented in a cinematic format, as a personal narrative told in the present tense with minimal psychological interpretation."[12] As a result, this section is less academic and more dramatic than the rest of the text.

Zimbardo also includes transcripts of recordings of the experiment and segments from post-study interviews, which offer insightful evidence for many of his claims. One participant assigned as a guard described his experience: "My enjoyment in harassing and punishing prisoners was quite unnatural for me, because I tend to think of myself as being sympathetic to the injured, especially animals. I think that it was an outgrowth from my total freedom to rule the prisoners, I began to abuse my authority."[13] This participant's experience touches on the themes that Zimbardo championed: that in powerful situations, people's behavior may change in transformative, surprising, and even abusive ways.

NOTES

1   Philip Zimbardo, *The Lucifer Effect: Understanding How Good People Turn Evil* (New York: Random House, 2007), VII.

2   Zimbardo, *Lucifer*, 3.

3   Zimbardo, *Lucifer*, 10.

4   Zimbardo, *Lucifer*, 10.

5   Zimbardo, *Lucifer*, 229.

6   Zimbardo, *Lucifer*, 196.

7   Zimbardo, *Lucifer*, 352.

8   Zimbardo, *Lucifer*, 377.

9   Zimbardo, *Lucifer*, 378.

10 Zimbardo, *Lucifer*, 378.

11 Zimbardo, *Lucifer*, XII.

12 Zimbardo, *Lucifer*, XII.

13 Zimbardo, *Lucifer*, 187.

MODULE 6
SECONDARY IDEAS

KEY POINTS

- *The Lucifer Effect's* secondary ideas include an examination of the psychological and social mechanisms responsible for people's turn to evil, as well as Philip Zimbardo's prescriptions for avoiding those pitfalls.

- Zimbardo describes group-based factors, such as the psychological desire to feel accepted by groups and the effect of feeling anonymous in groups, as mechanisms that lead people towards evil. To act heroically instead, one must be aware of, and combat, such factors.

- He also introduces a new idea in this text, examining how wider systems often facilitate the types of situations that are conducive to evil, and he discusses how these factors have been relatively overlooked.

Other Ideas

Philip Zimbardo's *The Lucifer Effect* contains two secondary ideas:
- A particular set of psychological and social mechanisms that push people to commit evil acts. He details what he views as the most prominent mechanisms.
- By consciously resisting those factors, people can become heroes—acting "on behalf of others, when yet others are doing evil or doing nothing to stop it."[1]

In his search for the psychological and social mechanisms that lead people to evil, Zimbardo draws on five decades of social psychological* research. He concludes that there are two distinct sets of factors. The first can be thought of as group-based factors, such as the need to

> **❝** In contrast to the 'banality of evil,' which posits that ordinary people can be responsible for the most despicable acts of cruelty and degradation of their fellows, I posit the 'banality of heroism,' which unfurls the banner of the heroic Everyman and Everywoman, who heed the call to service to humanity when their time comes to act. **❞**
>
> Philip Zimbardo, *The Lucifer Effect: Understanding How Good People Turn Evil*

belong* and feel welcomed by a group. These group-based factors exist when there are at least two people, and they typically involve one or more people exerting an influence, such as peer pressure,* on others in the group. Zimbardo describes the power that these group-based factors wield, noting, "The imagined threat of being cast [out of one's group] can lead some people to do virtually anything to avoid their terrifying rejection."[2]

The second set can be thought of as anonymity factors, which Zimbardo says are "anything, or any situation, that makes people feel anonymous, as though no one knows who they are or cares to know."[3] The effect of such factors, he continues, reduces people's "sense of personal accountability, thereby creating the potential for evil action."[4] This effect is exemplified by communications over the Internet, which being often anonymous, can typically be less civil and more antagonistic than face-to-face communications.

Zimbardo's other secondary idea is that people can avoid these pitfalls just as, according to him, heroes do. In addition to viewing most people as capable of evil, he also thinks most people are capable of heroism. Referencing a phrase descriptive of the capacity for "normal" people to perform "evil" acts in a routine fashion, Zimbardo writes: "The banality of evil shares much with the banality of heroism.

Neither attribute is the direct consequence of unique dispositional*
tendencies."[5] A person's individual characteristics, in other words, do not
necessarily have too much to do with his or her capacity to act in an evil
or heroic way. Instead, he argues, heroes manage to sidestep the group-
based and anonymity factors that often elicit evil in so many others.

Exploring the Ideas

According to Zimbardo, the first mechanisms that can elicit evil are
the group-based psychological factors. He considers that the need to
belong was a primary mechanism for the outcome of the Stanford
Prison Experiment (SPE), writing, "The basic need to belong, to
associate with and be accepted by others, so central to community
building and family bonding, was diverted in the SPE into
conformity* with newly emergent norms,* that enabled the guards
to abuse the prisoners."[6] In psychology, "norms" refer to the accepted
and expected standards, values, and ways to behave and think in any
given group, and are defined by the group itself. In this way,
Zimbardo explains that people are sometimes willing to forego their
own moral instincts if, in return, they are accepted into a group that
they wish, or feel obligated, to join.

In The *Lucifer Effect*, Zimbardo also considers other group-based
factors such as conformity and obedience to authority.* He references
the obedience studies* of the psychologist Stanley Milgram* in the
1960s as evidence of the profound effect that authorities have in
convincing others to obey their commands. In those studies, an
experimenter commanded study participants to provide simulated
electrical shocks to strangers who provided incorrect responses to
some task. Most participants in these Milgram studies administered the
highest available levels of shock, despite protestations from those being
shocked. Overall, such group-based factors involve a powerful leader
or the group's norms swaying group members to act in ways that go
against their personal moral standards.

The second set of mechanisms that Zimbardo says can elicit evil are factors serving anonymity.* "Deindividuation"* is a psychological phenomenon according to which people feel such a sense of anonymity in a wider group that they lose their sense of self-awareness and personal responsibility—leading to behaviors that would otherwise be out of character.

Meanwhile, dehumanization* involves deliberately overlooking or devaluing the humanity of another person (or group), usually viewing and treating the dehumanized as lesser, unequal, or animal. As Zimbardo describes, dehumanizing is excluding others "from the moral order of being a human person."[7] He notes that the two processes are often in play in situations that elicit evil. In the SPE, for instance, the guards addressed all the prisoners by numerical IDs instead of their names, which served to dehumanize them. Meanwhile, they themselves wore matching opaque sunglasses and uniforms, which deindividuated them.

Regarding heroes, Zimbardo writes that they do not have "some inherent magical goodness but rather, more likely, an understanding, however intuitive, of mental and social tactics of resistance."[8] So just as Zimbardo argues that nearly everyone is capable of evil, he similarly argues that nearly everyone is capable of heroism. But to be heroic, one must be aware of the psychological and social influences that often lead to evil and find methods to avoid them. For instance, being aware of—and consciously accepting your responsibility for—your actions or inactions will combat the effects of situations causing deindividuation.

Overlooked

Although *The Lucifer Effect* is a relatively recent book (published in 2007), much of the research and ideas it contains come from earlier works by Zimbardo and others. Zimbardo admits, however, that he and his colleagues in the field had previously overlooked the psychological effect of the system* (meaning larger organizations, governments, and cultures) on eliciting evil and failed to explore its high-level ability to impact every situation.

Speaking of broader systems, Zimbardo writes that "most psychologists have been insensitive to the deeper sources of power [inherent in] the political, economic, religious, historic, and cultural matrix that defines situations."[9] In his view, his academic peers were successful in examining how situations—such as a prison, school, church, or a simple collection of individuals—can influence behavior. But those researchers had consistently neglected to consider how such groups are created in the real world and the power that creators of such situations have.

For instance, in *The Lucifer Effect*, Zimbardo specifically blames US President George W. Bush,* Vice President Dick Cheney,* Defense Secretary Donald Rumsfeld,* and several other military leaders holding power at the time of the Abu Ghraib* prison abuses. He points out their role in establishing and enabling a culture that developed the "bad barrel"[10] that led to the torture at Abu Ghraib.

Previously, social psychologists have considered analyses at the level of the system to be generally outside the scope of their field, presuming them to be the remit of sociologists (those who study human society), political scientists (those who study the nature and actions of political systems and participants in those systems), and economists. Zimbardo's focus on systems is one of the newer ideas in *The Lucifer Effect*, so it remains to be seen to what extent psychologists will consider variables at the level of the system in the future—at least when examining the roots of situations that elicit unethical behavior.

NOTES

1   Philip Zimbardo, *The Lucifer Effect: Understanding How Good People Turn Evil* (New York: Random House, 2007), VIII.

2   Zimbardo, *Lucifer*, 259.

3   Zimbardo, *Lucifer*, 301.

4   Zimbardo, *Lucifer*, 301.

5   Zimbardo, *Lucifer*, 485.

6   Zimbardo, *Lucifer*, 258.

7   Zimbardo, *Lucifer*, 307.

8   Zimbardo, *Lucifer*, XIII.

9   Zimbardo, *Lucifer*, X.

10 Zimbardo, *Lucifer*, X.

MODULE 7
ACHIEVEMENT

KEY POINTS

- In *The Lucifer Effect*, Philip Zimbardo provides the most extensive telling and analysis of the Stanford Prison Experiment (SPE),* and he uses this analysis to explain the situational forces* involved in the Abu Ghraib* prison scandal.

- As the Abu Ghraib abuses and Zimbardo's involvement in the trial of one guard are both relatively recent events, the text is timely and revealing.

- The reliability of the SPE, and the universality of its findings, are difficult to demonstrate because ethical considerations largely prevent replication of the original study.

Assessing the Argument

In his review of Philip Zimbardo's *The Lucifer Effect: Understanding How Good People Turn Evil*, the social psychologist Robert Levine* asks, "Why a new book about a 35-year-old study?"[1] He answers his own question, writing, "[Zimbardo] provides a wealth of new interpretations and new material—anecdotes, entries from the diaries of prisoners and guards, updates on the lives of the participants, and documentation of the consequences his findings have had for real-world prison policy."[2]

Examples are Zimbardo's presentations of his findings directly to judicial and law enforcement groups as well as his testimony in court, arguing that solitary confinement* of prisoners is psychologically damaging and abusive.

Although Zimbardo's analyses of heroism and how systemic factors (such as governments) enable powerful situations are somewhat less comprehensive, they nevertheless provide a valuable starting point

> ❝ Drawing on path-breaking experimental work conducted in the 1970s in the Stanford Prison Experiment, Zimbardo brilliantly examines the current Abu Ghraib prison torture scandal. He meticulously details the situational factors which can make good people engage in evil acts, in order to meet natural and normal human needs for safety, knowledge, and affection. ❞
>
> Rose McDermott, *Reviewed Work: The Lucifer Effect: Understanding How Good People Turn Evil by Philip Zimbardo*

for further investigation. Zimbardo notes in *The Lucifer Effect* that social psychologists have largely ignored the topics of heroism and systemic influences on behavior, and he hopes he can stimulate future research on the topics. Levine praised Zimbardo's work on heroism and his nuanced definition and categorization of heroic thought and behaviors, adding that he hoped it "will stimulate long-overdue research and education in this area."[3]

Although the topic remains largely ignored by researchers, Zimbardo is doing his part to educate the world with his Heroic Imagination Project (HIP),* a public training program that teaches people how to avoid potential pitfalls that prevent heroic acts. Those include deindividuation* (the loss of a sense of one's own self and tendencies due to inclusion in a group or because of one's anonymity), dehumanization* (overlooking or devaluing the human attributes of another person), and conformity* (matching one's thought and behavior to that of a group due to things such as social pressure).

Achievement in Context
Although the SPE study is more than three decades old, the events at Abu Ghraib acted as an impetus for Zimbardo and made a retelling of

the study more relevant and instructive than ever. In her review of *The Lucifer Project*, the political scientist Rose McDermott* said that the SPE remains "hauntingly relevant upon the release of the photos from Abu Ghraib prison some 30 years later."[4] She noted that the text "contains many photos from the original experiment, and they will strike any viewer as startlingly familiar in design to the more recent Abu Ghraib pictures. Some of the poses in which guards placed prisoners reemerge as identical in nature and scope."[5]

Even the 2004 Schlesinger report,* the independent report of the Abu Ghraib abuses that was commissioned by the US Department of Defense (DoD), noted the relevance, stating, "The landmark Stanford study provides a cautionary tale for all military detention operations."[6] Some observers may have expected that the Schlesinger report would influence US policy on the treatment of foreign military prisoners and terror suspects, given the report's official status and the amount of media attention it attracted. However, later reports (including one of 2010 by Amnesty International,* an organization founded to defend the human rights of political prisoners) found that the US government's abuse and torture of detainees continued in other prisons for years after the publication of the Schlesinger report and *The Lucifer Effect*. Abu Ghraib, however, was closed in 2008.

Limitations

The psychologist Stanley Milgram's* obedience studies* and Zimbardo's SPE most vividly demonstrate the possible magnitude of unexpected and evil behaviors. However, they are not often replicated because of ethical considerations, as they both placed participants in scenarios that are today deemed too psychologically stressful to repeat. Thus, it is difficult to prove the universality of the power of situations.

Social psychologists have also noted that people's perceptions of the power of situations are culturally variable. Zimbardo writes in his text: "The traditional view (among those who come from cultures that emphasize individualism)* is to look within for answers—for pathology or heroism. Modern psychiatry is dispositionally* oriented."[7] In other words, in some "individualist" cultures, such as in Western countries like the United States, people tend to think of themselves as individuals more than as members of a group. As a result, they generally tend to attribute the cause of events to innate personality factors (or "dispositions.") Therefore, it's assumed that a person's aggressive act is most likely evidence that he or she is an aggressive person rather than the result of some situational factor.

Zimbardo points out that a willingness to assume the "bad apple" explanation for unethical acts might vary by culture, with American and Western culture in particular likely to rely on the bad apple attributions. In non-Western cultures, such as in East Asia, people are often more attuned to situational factors and the influence they have on people's lives. The consequence of this is that Western, individualist cultures, at least according to Zimbardo's view, are less likely to notice and question authorities that may be enabling bad situations, like their government or their boss.

An additional limitation to the text is Zimbardo's reluctance to define what he means by "evil." He instead provides many examples of what he considers to be evil—from the guards' behaviors during the SPE and at Abu Ghraib to cases of financial fraud, genocide, and sexual abuse. Zimbardo notes that he views evil as broader than what in his opinion is typically described as such, and he writes that it is more than "political leaders who have orchestrated mass murders."[8] It seems that Zimbardo intends to consider evil as a broad category with unclear boundaries. But he does not address in the text the likelihood that different people and societies will differ in what they consider evil.

NOTES

1   Robert Levine, "The Evil That Men Do," *American Scientist*, September–October 2007, accessed September 15, 2015, http://www.americanscientist.org/bookshelf/content2/2007/5/the-evil-that-men-do.

2   Robert Levine, "The Evil That Men Do."

3   Robert Levine, "The Evil That Men Do."

4   McDermott, "Reviewed Work," 645.

5   McDermott, "Reviewed Work," 645.

6   Philip Zimbardo, *The Lucifer Effect: Understanding How Good People Turn Evil* (New York: Random House, 2007), 324.

7   Zimbardo, *Lucifer*, 7.

8   Zimbardo, *Lucifer*, 6.

PLACE IN THE AUTHOR'S WORK

KEY POINTS

- One of Philip Zimbardo's interests lies in examining when and how people act unexpectedly. In the 1971 Stanford Prison Experiment (SPE)* and *The Lucifer Effect* (2007), this involves supposedly ordinary people acting out evil.

- Though his research based on the SPE has laid out a prototype for the power of the situation,* Zimbardo's other work has been more reliant on dispositional* factors— those associated with the individual's personality.

- The publication of *The Lucifer Effect*, however, has reignited the original debates prompted by the SPE during the 1970s. As a result, the book has reaffirmed Zimbardo's reputation for research on situations.

Positioning

Published in 2007, *The Lucifer Effect: Understanding How Good People Turn Evil* is a late publication in Philip Zimbardo's career. However, it relies on work conducted during the early stages of his career and serves as a return to the research topics with which he has been most associated: the power of the situation, evil behavior, and the dynamics and psychological consequences of imprisonment. Relatively new in *The Lucifer Effect* is Zimbardo's consideration of systemic* factors and his focus on heroism* through avoiding negative situational forces.*

Zimbardo admits in the book that for much of his career, he overlooked the influence of systems such as institutions. In an interview, he noted that he was "unaware even with the Stanford prison study about the power of the system, because I was the system."[1] He says that he only had this realization while serving as expert

> **❝** At the core of my interest is the process of transformation of human nature. What factors account for how we suddenly change, how we act in ways that are not based on what we did before, or on what we thought we knew about ourselves and about other people? **❞**
>
> Philip Zimbardo, *Emperor of the Edge*

witness for the American soldier Ivan Frederick,* accused of mistreating detainees at the Abu Ghraib* prison in 2004.

Above all, *The Lucifer Effect* marks Zimbardo's transition toward what has since become his primary focus: heroism. Although he only discusses heroism in a short section of the book, it has served as a catalyst for his later focus on heroism. In 2010, Zimbardo launched the Heroic Imagination Project, (HIP)* which trains interested participants to resist negative situational factors. He writes that this "lies in development of the three Ss: self-awareness, situational sensitivity, and street smarts."[2] All three involve first understanding the power of negative situational factors, such as deindividuation* and conformity* and then thinking about how one might react to those pressures. Thus, the premise of Zimbardo's HIP had its origins in *The Lucifer Effect*.

Integration

Although Zimbardo remains most associated with the SPE and a "situationist"* school of thought (focusing on the power of the situation), he has covered a range of research topics throughout his career. In fact, he describes himself as a generalist in psychology rather than a specialist in any one area. Nonetheless, some broad themes run through his body of work.

In one interview, he described his core interest, saying, "I have been primarily interested in how and why ordinary people do unusual things, things that seem alien to their natures."[3] Two of his other key research interests have been shyness and the perception of time. In his work on shyness, Zimbardo strives to help shy people overcome their lack of confidence and, in a sense, behave in ways that are unusual for them. However, counter to the stance found in *The Lucifer Effect* and his other research on evil, Zimbardo's shyness work tends to focus more on dispositions. He sees shyness as a personality variable, or the result of thinking styles, rather than the result of situational factors alone.

Zimbardo's research on time perspective also provides additional nuance to his body of work. It details how a person's emphasis—or overemphasis—on events of the past, possibilities for the future, or living in the present moment can affect their behaviors. This work is what psychologists might call interactionist* as it considers that the *interaction* between a person's personality and the situation is a better predictor of behavior than either the personality element or the situation element on its own.

Zimbardo explicitly regards time perspective in this way, writing that he considers it "as situationally determined and as a relatively stable individual–differences process."[4] (More simply put, he means that both situational and dispositional factors are integral to people's perception of time.) As a result, although Zimbardo's position as a situationist is obvious in his writings on the SPE and *The Lucifer Effect,* his work in social psychology* has been more varied and nuanced, including both dispositional and interactionist ideas.

Significance

Based on two key events to which Zimbardo had unique access, *The Lucifer Effect* is probably his most extensive and detailed work, as well as most widely accessible text. It also assigns more blame and offers up more prescriptions than any of his previous works, largely directed at the US military and government. For instance, Zimbardo assigns specific blame to former US President George W. Bush* and Secretary of Defense Donald Rumsfeld* for their roles in establishing a large-scale system that ultimately dehumanized* Iraqis (that is, robbed them of their status as human beings).

The Lucifer Effect has further cemented Zimbardo's association with the SPE and his position as a situationist. Both have been controversial topics since Zimbardo's original work in the 1970s, and this text has reignited some of those debates—with Zimbardo again becoming a central and polarizing figure. While the SPE is held as one of the most famous, interesting and possibly informative studies in the field, it is also regarded as one of the most unethical. Zimbardo has acknowledged this many times in his career, including in *The Lucifer Effect*, in which he asks the question: "Was the SPE unethical? In several ways, the answer must surely be 'Yes.'"[5]

Nonetheless, Zimbardo qualifies his admission, arguing that the study was not unethical by other standards. He also claims the presumed suffering of the SPE participants was acceptable and worthwhile. While the text provides much new detail into one of the field's seminal studies as well as new ideas about systemic factors and heroism, it has also vaulted Zimbardo back into a debate over ethics in the field. For some observers, this invariably colors his reputation.

NOTES

1 Marina Krakovsky, "Zimbardo Unbound," *Stanford Magazine,* May/June 2007, accessed September 27, 2015, https://alumni.stanford.edu/get/page/magazine/article/?article_id=32541.

2 Philip Zimbardo, *The Lucifer Effect: Understanding How Good People Turn Evil* (New York: Random House, 2007), 452.

3   Christina Maslach, "Emperor of the Edge," *Psychology Today*, September 1, 2000, accessed September 15, 2015, https://www.psychologytoday.com/articles/200009/emperor-the-edge.

4   Philip G. Zimbardo, and John N. Boyd, "Putting Time in Perspective: A Valid, Reliable Individual-Differences Metric." *Journal of Personality and Social Psychology* 77, no. 6 (1999): 1272.

5   Zimbardo, *Lucifer*, 231.

SECTION 3
IMPACT

THE FIRST RESPONSES

KEY POINTS

- The prominent feature of Philip Zimbardo's *The Lucifer Effect*, the Stanford Prison Experiment (SPE),* has long been criticized as unethical and methodologically suspect.

- Zimbardo concedes that the SPE included lapses in ethical practice; however he defends his original analysis of the study against methodological critiques.

- The SPE became a seminal case study in ethics for the field, and the 2007 release of *The Lucifer Effect* reignited debate over Zimbardo's interpretation of the study's results.

Criticism

Because Philip Zimbardo's *The Lucifer Effect: Understanding How Good People Turn Evil* relies so heavily on the Stanford Prison Experiment, criticisms of the text mostly reflect the original criticisms of the 1971 study. These tend to focus on two main concerns: ethics and methodology. One 1973 reviewer was particularly critical regarding the ethics of the study, claiming that participants were not provided with enough accurate information in advance to consent to the experiment and that their suffering was not justified.

Nearly four decades later, a reviewer of *The Lucifer Effect* noted that the SPE was "now used as a case study of research ethics gone awry."[1] Zimbardo's SPE participants endured more psychological distress than most social scientists felt was acceptable. Critics also argued that because Zimbardo acted as superintendent of the makeshift prison, he was unable to objectively monitor the condition and safety of participants.

> 66 Was the SPE [Stanford Prison Experiment]* study
> unethical? No and Yes. No, because it followed the
> guidelines of the Human Subjects Research Review
> Board* that reviewed it and approved it ... Yes, it was
> unethical because people suffered and others were
> allowed to inflict pain and humiliation on their fellows
> over an extended period of time. 99
>
> Philip Zimbardo et al., *Reflections on the Stanford Prison Experiment:*
> *Genesis, Transformations, Consequences*

In the first years after the SPE, criticisms of its methodology focused on alternative explanations for the events that took place. Many people believed that the participants' behaviors were not as organic as Zimbardo suggested. A common critique was that of political scientist Ali Banuazizi* and the sociologist* Siamak Movahedi.* In 1975, they wrote that demand characteristics* were largely responsible for the events that took place during the SPE.

The term "demand characteristics" refers to a situation where participants form their own interpretation of the purpose of the experiment or the expectations of the experimenter. Thus, feeling an implicit pressure to perform as expected, they subconsciously change their behavior to fit that interpretation. This creates a bias in the results and serious questions about the validity of any observed effects.

Banuazizi and Movahedi argued that the participants probably uncovered Zimbardo's hypothesis and expectations for the study, and they may have adapted their behaviors to please him. Banuazizi and Movahedi noted that "the subjects entered the experiment carrying strong social stereotypes of how guards and prisoners act and relate to one another in a real prison,"[2] and they essentially acted out those roles.

Responses

Since the publication of *The Lucifer Effect*, Zimbardo seems to have avoided making any public responses to such criticisms. In 2007, he published a short post on his website to those with any concerns over the book's conclusions or any renewed doubts about the SPE's methodology, writing: "I do not have the time nor the inclination to enter into any further discussion or debate about this matter."[3] He probably did not consider it worthwhile to repeat the stance that he had provided in previous years, particularly as *The Lucifer Effect* included the original responses to these criticisms.

For instance, Zimbardo had conceded in 1973 that in some ways the study was unethical. But he also defended himself on several grounds, noting that he had gained approval from several institutional review boards* to conduct the study. He also argued that he debriefed* his participants many times (in a post-study discussion which gives participants additional information about the study and checks for any psychological strain). Zimbardo noted that he disclosed the true intent of the work and was "sufficiently convinced that the suffering we observed, and were responsible for, was stimulus-bound [that is, a specific behavior that occurs as a response to a specific stimuli] and did not extend beyond the confines of that basement prison."[4]

He repeats those arguments in *The Lucifer Effect*, saying that while, in absolute terms, the study was unethical, enough was learned from it to warrant the strain it placed on its participants. Zimbardo declares: "On the relativist side of the ethical argument [that is, making judgments based on the relative value of costs and benefits, rather than on absolute truths or values], one could contend that the SPE was not unethical."[5]

However, Zimbardo does admit in the book that some demand characteristics were likely to be present. He writes about his own role adoption and acting during the study, noting: "In retrospect, my role transformation from usually compassionate teacher to data-focused researcher to callous prison superintendent was most distressing."[6]

Zimbardo, however, offers a different interpretation. He contends that this only further illustrates the power of the situation*—in that it changed even him—rather than being evidence that he or the participants were intentionally acting out roles.

Conflict and Consensus

In response to the immediate criticisms of the SPE in 1971 and those that have continued up to—and even after—the publication of *The Lucifer Effect*, Zimbardo has stuck to his original interpretation of the SPE's findings and maintained the same responses to questions about the study's ethics. There seems to be little movement on the side of Zimbardo's critics, as well. They consider the SPE, alongside Stanley Milgrim's* 1960s obedience studies,* as social psychology's* prime examples of unethical research.

In their influential 2012 handbook on research ethics, the psychologist Joan E. Sieber* and sociologist Martin B. Tolich* argue that "Zimbardo's ethical problem stemmed from… [his] conflict of interest as a researcher … and a co-subject in his role as prison superintendent."[7] They write that the SPE is now informative, suggesting: "All researchers can take lessons from this conflict of interest. Researchers … need to monitor the study and the subjects at all times."[8] In other words, they maintain that, as prison superintendent, Zimbardo could not objectively monitor the safety of the study participants and, on that point, Zimbardo agrees.

Questions over both the role of demand characteristics in the SPE study and challenges to the interpretations of Zimbardo's analysis have also persisted, although no consensus has been reached. Zimbardo continues to defend his original interpretation of the SPE and now its application to other events, such as the Abu Ghraib* prison abuses. Meanwhile, the release of *The Lucifer Effect* has caused renewed interest in finding alternative explanations for the SPE.

NOTES

1   Wray Herbert, "The Banality of Evil," *Observer*, April 2007, accessed September 27, 2015, http://aps.psychologicalscience.org/index.php/publications/observer/2007/april-07/the-banality-of-evil.html.

2   Ali Banuazizi and Siamak Movahedi, "Interpersonal Dynamics in a Simulated Prison: A Methodological Analysis," *American Psychologist* 30, no. 2 (1975): 156.

3   Philip Zimbardo, "Person X Situation X System Dynamics," *The Lucifer Effect*, accessed September 27, 2015, http://www.lucifereffect.com/apsrejoinder.htm.

4   Philip G. Zimbardo, "On the Ethics of Intervention in Human Psychological Research: With Special Reference to the Stanford Prison Experiment," *Cognition* 2, no. 2 (1973): 254.

5   Philip Zimbardo, *The Lucifer Effect: Understanding How Good People Turn Evil* (New York: Random House, 2007), 263.

6   Zimbardo, *Lucifer*, 218.

7   Joan E. Sieber and Martin B. Tolich, *Planning Ethically Responsible Research* (Thousand Oaks: Sage Publications, 2012), 67.

8   Sieber and Tolich, *Responsible*, 67.

MODULE 10
THE EVOLVING DEBATE

KEY POINTS

- *The Lucifer Effect* provides arguments and evidence that certain settings, such as US prisons, are likely to be home to abuse, sadism,* and evil.

- *The Lucifer Effect* established a school of thought that bad situations create bad people. Another school of thought countered that it is bad people in a situation that make it bad.

- The Stanford Prison Experiment (SPE)* and *The Lucifer Effect* have particularly influenced research on prison settings.

Uses and Problems

The ideas found in Philip Zimbardo's 2007 *The Lucifer Effect: Understanding How Good People Turn Evil* have influenced academic literature on prison policy. The social psychologist* Craig Haney* argues that evidence from the SPE and other prison research demonstrates that, "because of their harmful potential, prisons should be deployed very sparingly in the war on crime."[1] A psychology professor at the University of California, Santa Cruz, Haney is renowned for his work on the psychological effects of incarceration and the effectiveness of prisons. The crux of his argument is that if prisons have the capability to alter people's behavior, as demonstrated by the SPE, this power ought to be used to rehabilitate inmates. Yet, as the SPE and other prison research has documented, prisons are instead more likely to dehumanize* and even psychologically torture inmates.

> **❝** The potential for significant abuse [is inherent in] the very structure of a prison. Whatever its limitations as a literal simulation of an actual prison setting, the venerable Stanford Prison Experiment demonstrated the potentially destructive dynamic that is created whenever near absolute power is wielded over a group of derogated [that is, insulted and treated as worthless] and vilified others. **❞**
>
> Craig Haney, *A Culture of Harm Taming the Dynamics of Cruelty in Supermax Prisons*

Despite its influence on prison policy, the release of *The Lucifer Effect* also led to the continuation of—and increase in—concerns surrounding Zimbardo's methodology and interpretation of the SPE. In 2001, Stephen Reicher* and S. Alexander Haslam,* both social psychologists and psychology professors, conducted one notable study in collaboration with the BBC* (the British Broadcasting Corporation). The researchers randomly split 15 participants into prisoner and guard groups in a makeshift detention center. This was not, however, a replication of the SPE—partly because it would be forbidden by modern ethics. In this instance, Reicher and Haslam reported that guards were "reluctant to impose their authority and they were eventually overcome by the prisoners."[2] The remainder of the study included participants attempting to form an egalitarian* structure, where all people are treated equally, by fairly delegating various tasks and chores. But this approach failed and was supplanted by efforts to reestablish a guard–prisoner hierarchy.

Schools of Thought

This BBC prison study* and other alternative explanations of the SPE have led to a more nuanced school of thought on the power of situations.* Zimbardo has advocated a cause-and-effect process, arguing that difficult situations and systems (bad barrels) create bad apples. But the BBC prison study suggests that powerful situations such as prisons descending into sadism and evil are less inevitable than Zimbardo suggests.

Reicher and Haslam argue that "the way in which members of strong groups behave depends upon the norms* and values associated with their specific social identity and may be either anti- or prosocial."[3] This argument suggests, in part, that Zimbardo developed and enabled a situation in the SPE prison that promoted abuse, and that Zimbardo, more than the situational factors he detailed, was responsible for the outcomes of the SPE.

Further work has suggested that it is more likely that "bad apples" create the "bad barrels." In 2007, psychology professors Thomas Carnahan* and Sam McFarland* conducted a study that aimed to examine the personality characteristics of people who respond to recruitment materials requesting participants for a prison study. They found that "volunteers who responded to a newspaper ad to participate in a psychological study of prison life, an ad virtually identical to that used in the Stanford Prison Experiment,"[4] were higher on several measures of aggression and had a greater tendency to support authority and social dominance than people responding to a hypothetical study with a parallel advert omitting the words "prison life."[5]

This school of thought fits into the interactionist* category, as it not only gives similar weight to personality* and situational* factors in determining behavior but it also suggests that the interaction between certain personalities in certain situations can be better predictors of behavior than personalities or situations on their own. Those personalities are, for example, people with authoritarian* personalities—those given to the exercise of their authority—in a strongly hierarchical systems like a prison.

In Current Scholarship

In addition to the academic debates in the fields of social and personality psychology* that the text has spurred, Craig Haney—one of Zimbardo's former students who acted as a key researcher during the SPE—has become a leading voice in prison research and prison policy. Haney wrote in 2008 that "we have reached the upper limit of the psychological, social, economic, and even cultural costs that our society can afford to incur in the name of this commitment to inflicting penal pain."[6] His conclusions are based on decades of research that largely began with his involvement in the SPE and are in line with Zimbardo's analysis of the SPE and its implications for prison policy.

Haney has found that the psychological strain and suffering that occurred during the SPE is much worse in actual prisons. This suffering is due to many factors that were apparent in the SPE, such as the isolation of prisoners, power abuses in prisons, and the emphasis on punishment rather than rehabilitation.

Starting in the 1970s, the US began a "'get tough' approach to crime control,"[7] with the expansion of prisons and lengthening of prison sentences. Haney writes that these prison policies and practices have since "crossed the line from inflicting pain to doing real harm—at a societal as well as individual level."[8] America incarcerates a significant segment of the population, and rather than rehabilitating criminals, the system does them additional psychological harm before sending them back into society at the end of their prison sentence.

NOTES

1   Craig Haney and Philip Zimbardo, "The Past and Future of US Prison Policy: Twenty-five Years after the Stanford Prison Experiment." *American Psychologist* 53, no. 7 (1998): 719.

2   Stephen Reicher and S. Alexander Haslam, "Rethinking the Psychology of Tyranny: The BBC Prison Study." *British Journal of Social Psychology* 45, no. 1 (2006): 1.

3   Reicher and Haslam, "Tyranny," 33.

4   Thomas Carnahan and Sam McFarland, "Revisiting the Stanford Prison Experiment: Could Participant Self-Selection Have Led to the Cruelty?" *Personality and Social Psychology Bulletin* 33, no. 5 (2007): 610.

5   Carnahan and McFarland, "Revisiting," 610.

6   Craig Haney, "Counting Casualties in the War on Prisoners." *USFL* Rev. 43 (2008): 89.

7   Haney, "Prisoners," 88.

8   Haney, "Prisoners," 89.

IMPACT AND INFLUENCE TODAY

KEY POINTS

- *The Lucifer Effect* today serves as the best record of the famous Stanford Prison Experiment (SPE).* It stands as a source of renewed controversy over both the SPE and the influence of situational forces* in eliciting unethical behavior. It is also the primary source for Philip Zimbardo's more recent ideas on systemic* causes of both behavior and heroism.*

- Zimbardo has since not participated in the ongoing debate over reinterpretations of the SPE and the power of situations.* Instead he has focused his attention on new work, primarily on heroism.

- Both social psychologists* and personality psychologists* continue to debate the power of situations to elicit unethical behavior.

Position

Philip Zimbardo's *The Lucifer Effect: Understanding How Good People Turn Evil* (2007) is the most comprehensive telling and analysis of the 1971 Stanford Prison Experiment to date. As such, it is historically relevant for the field of social psychology and is likely to remain so for some time.

The inclusion of so much new information on the SPE has also provided both sides with new material to debate. This includes previously unreleased transcripts from the study, photographs, and descriptions of video footage. In one post-study interview, a guard summarized his surprise at his behavior: "[When] a prisoner reacted violently toward me, I found that I had to defend myself, not as me but

> ❝ Bad apples vs. bad barrels' was the wrong way to frame this discussion. The metaphor oversimplifies a complex and troubling reality, which is that there is plenty of blame to go around. ❞
>
> George R. Mastroianni, *Looking Back: Understanding Abu Ghraib*

as me the guard … He hated me as the guard. He was reacting to the uniform. I had no choice but to defend myself as a guard."[1]

Such insights provide evidence for several of Zimbardo's contentions, such as people's adoption of roles (here as a guard) and their ability to deindividuate* (here the guard implying that the "true him" was not hated; it was "the guard").

To date, most attention to the text has focused on the continued debate over the power of situations and differing interpretations of the SPE. But some conversations now focus on the two newer topics contained in *The Lucifer Effect*. The first is Zimbardo's claim that wider systems produced the various bad situations described in the book. The second is his analysis of heroism as resulting from an awareness of, and ability to avoid, the pressures and pitfalls of bad situations.

These points reposition Zimbardo, who has moved away from his earlier work on the SPE, and they also involve new prescriptions and a new audience. Reviewing the book, the political scientist* Rose McDermott* summarized it as encouraging readers to resist "the subtle ways politicians and others use the environment to manipulate unsuspecting bystanders into doing their dirty work for them."[2] The idea, as promoted by Zimbardo, is that there is value in people questioning the intentions of their governments.

Interaction

Zimbardo remains the most prominent voice promoting the ideas found in *The Lucifer Effect*. In recent years, he has apparently chosen to not get involved in the debate over the methodology of his work and the degree of situational factors at play in events such as the SPE and Abu Ghraib.* In 2007, Zimbardo stated on his website that these debates distract from the factors he hoped to focus on in *The Lucifer Effect*. He wrote that "while personality and social psychologists spar about the relative contributions of dispositions* and situations, we have ignored the most significant factor in the behavioral equation—the System."[3]

Thus, Zimbardo seems to be focusing now on the most recent of his themes in *The Lucifer Effect*: the effects of systems on human behavior and on heroism. This is a recent challenge to the fields of social psychology and personality psychology, with Zimbardo considering that enough work has been done on the power of situations and hoping to move into more positive, and applied, work on heroism. In a 2011 article, he wrote: "What makes us good? What makes us evil? Research has uncovered many answers to the second question … But when we ask why people become heroic, research doesn't yet have an answer."[4] It seems that, following *The Lucifer Effect*, Zimbardo has quickly shifted his focus from the predictors of evil to the predictors of heroism.

The Continuing Debate

However, those challenged by Zimbardo have not abandoned the debate over the influence of situational factors. In 2007, dozens of social and personality psychologists, several among the most respected in the world, wrote a letter to the Association for Psychological Science,* a major American psychology research organization, voicing concerns over *The Lucifer Effect*. "In contrast to Zimbardo," they wrote, "we believe that there is actually little scientific evidence indicating that situations are more important than dispositions for explaining behavior."[5] They also questioned the likelihood of Zimbardo's situational account of the abuses at Abu Ghraib.

Similarly, in a reanalysis of the SPE and Stanley Milgram's obedience studies,* the social psychologists Stephen Reicher* and S.

Alexander Haslam* filmed a documentary reinterpretation of the SPE with volunteers that was broadcast on the British Broadcasting Corporation (BBC).* They maintained that a large body of research did not support the idea that situations can lead a majority of people to conform to evil.

Reicher and Haslam argued that the persistent "situationist"* idea ignores evidence that many people do resist the situational forces that Zimbardo described, and that those who do give in to situational pressures and "heed authority in doing evil do so knowingly not blindly, actively not passively, creatively not automatically … In short, they should be seen—and judged—as engaged followers not as blind conformists."[6] Thus, Reicher and Haslam contended that it is not ordinary people who are swayed by situations to evil, as Zimbardo argues, but rather people with a propensity for evil who are swayed by the situation.

NOTES

1 Philip Zimbardo, *The Lucifer Effect: Understanding How Good People Turn Evil* (New York: Random House, 2007), 189.

2 Rose McDermott, "Reviewed Work: *The Lucifer Effect: Understanding How Good People Turn Evil* by Philip Zimbardo," Political Psychology 28, No. 5 (2007): 646.

3 Philip Zimbardo, "Person X Situation X System Dynamics," *The Lucifer Effect*, accessed September 27, 2015, http://www.lucifereffect.com/apsrejoinder.htm.

4 Philip Zimbardo, "What Makes a Hero?" *Greater Good Science Center*, January 18, 2011, accessed September 27, 2015, http://greatergood.berkeley.edu/article/item/what_makes_a_hero/.

5 M. Brent Donnellan et al., "Not So Situational," *Observer*, June/July 2007, accessed September 27, 2015, http://www.psychologicalscience.org/index.php/publications/observer/2007/june-july-07/not-so-situational.html.

6 S. Alexander Haslam and Stephen D. Reicher, "Contesting the 'Nature' Of Conformity: What Milgram and Zimbardo's Studies Really Show," *PLoS Biology* 10, no. 11 (2012): 1.

WHERE NEXT?

KEY POINTS

- *The Lucifer Effect* is likely to continue spurring controversy over interpretations of the Stanford Prison Experiment (SPE)* and the power of situations* to elicit unethical behavior. However, it also has the potential to serve as an inspiration for new work on heroism.*

- In the near future, Philip Zimbardo is most likely to carry out this potential through missions such as his Heroic Imagination Project.*

- The text is seminal for many reasons, including its dramatic and extensive retelling of one of psychology's most famed studies.

Potential

Philip Zimbardo's 1971 Stanford Prison Experiment and his 2007 book, *The Lucifer Effect: Understanding How Good People Turn Evil*, will continue to serve as a case study for research ethics and as a centerpiece in the debate over the situational determinants of behaviors. "Psychologists will find a wealth of fascinating new information in a nearly hour-by-hour account of the Stanford study,"[1] writes the psychology professor George R. Mastroianni.* He also suggests that "Zimbardo has made a major contribution to the field by including this new information, which will hopefully stimulate a significant reconsideration of the lessons of the Stanford study."[2]

Indeed, the few years since the text's release have seen a renewed focus on the SPE and even on Stanley Milgram's* related obedience studies.* Though this renewed debate was not Zimbardo's intent with the book, and he has expressed disappointment over its persistence, the debate has already resulted in a more nuanced perspective of evil.

> ❝Building on these insights, I have helped to start a program designed to learn more of heroism and to create the heroes of tomorrow. ❞
>
> Philip Zimbardo, *What Makes a Hero?*

Zimbardo has been able to apply his ideas on heroism, and this work is likely to expand in the coming years. Chief among such early applications is a nonprofit organization that he established, the Heroic Imagination Project (HIP), which intends to teach "people how to take effective action in challenging situations."[3] Zimbardo has written that this project aims to conduct and encourage future research into the topic of heroism as well as to provide "research-based education and training programs for middle and high schools, corporations, and the military that make people aware of the social factors that produce passivity, inspire them to take positive civic action, and encourage the skills needed to consistently translate heroic impulses into action."[4]

Future Directions

Zimbardo continues today as the most vocal, visible, and prominent thinker promoting the power of the situation*—specifically its ability to lead ordinary people to commit evil and to therefore serve as an explanation for many historical atrocities. He is also likely to continue as the most visible researcher promoting the ideas of heroism found in the text.

However, one of his former students, the clinical psychologist Zeno Franco,* has researched the topic of heroism alongside Zimbardo and is now an advisor to Zimbardo's Heroic Imagination Project. Writing in 2006, Franco wrote that having a "heroic imagination"[5] was an early candidate as a predictor and determinant of heroism, which he defined as "the capacity to imagine facing physically or socially risky situations, to struggle with the hypothetical problems these situations generate, and to consider one's actions and the consequences."[6] In essence, thinking through these possibilities before they occur can better prepare people for when they do occur.

Meanwhile, the social psychologist Craig Haney* is likely to continue researching US prison policies and advocating for prison reform. Many social scientists who are researching prisons acknowledge that US policy leaders have largely discounted their work. Yet Haney remains optimistic that both his research and the broader evidence from both prison research and social psychology* will eventually influence US public and political opinion about the role of prisons in society. He wrote in his 2005 book that the costs of the US policy of mass incarceration* is "beginning to register and mount in significant and unsettling ways in many communities across the country … there is a growing sense that it is time to seriously rethink what we have done."[7] Haney and other prison policy researchers typically hope for an approach to criminal justice that more effectively rehabilitates criminals, avoids the psychological damage associated with current US prisons, and does so for less money than the current rate of mass incarceration requires.

Summary

The Lucifer Effect offers the most readable and extensive report of one of the most famous psychology studies, the Stanford Prison Experiment. This alone makes it a valuable read for students. Yet the text offers much more, including a detailed analysis of many powerful social and group pressures, such as conformity* and deindividualization,* that are integral to understanding Zimbardo's take on the power of the situation. Even if a reader is skeptical of this power, the phenomena that Zimbardo presents are crucial to understanding the field of social psychology. And because such forces have the potential to influence behavior in ways that most people find objectionable, many people should find the book enlightening.

It offers insights into tragic events such as Abu Ghraib* that many readers might otherwise have difficultly comprehending.

The American social psychologist Robert Levine* suggested that "This important book should be required reading not only for social scientists, but also for politicians, decision-makers, educators and just about anyone else disturbed by the self-destructive directions in which the United States and the rest of the world seem to be moving."[8] Levine, like Zimbardo, hopes that knowledge of situational factors will make people less susceptible to their ill effects.

Yet Zimbardo's final message is optimistic and meant as a call to action for general readers: "Each of us may possess the capacity to do terrible things. But we also possess an inner hero; if stirred to action, that inner hero is capable of performing tremendous goodness for others."[9]

NOTES

1   George R. Mastroianni, "Zimbardo's Apple." *Analyses of Social Issues and Public Policy* 7, no. 1 (2007): 251.

2   Mastroianni, "Zimbardo's Apple," 251.

3   What is HIP?" Heroic Imagination Project, accessed September 27, 2015, http://heroicimagination.org/.

4   Philip Zimbardo, "What Makes a Hero?" *Greater Good Science Center*, January 18, 2011, accessed September 27, 2015, http://greatergood.berkeley.edu/article/item/what_makes_a_hero.

5   Zeno Franco and Philip Zimbardo, "The Banality of Heroism," *Greater Good Science Center*, September 1, 2006, accessed September 27, 2015, http://greatergood.berkeley.edu/article/item/the_banality_of_heroism.

6   Franco and Zimbardo, "The Banality of Heroism."

7   Craig Haney, *Reforming Punishment: Psychological Limits to the Pains of Imprisonment.* (Washington DC: American Psychological Association, 2006), x.

8   Robert Levine, "The Evil That Men Do," *American Scientist*, September-October 2007, accessed September 15, 2015, http://www.americanscientist.org/bookshelf/content2/2007/5/the-evil-that-men-do.

9   Zimbardo, "What Makes a Hero?"

GLOSSARY

GLOSSARY OF TERMS

Abu Ghraib: a prison in Baghdad where Iraqi prisoners and detainees were held captive during the American-led 2003 invasion of Iraq. A scandal erupted after it was revealed that the prisoners there were subjected to physical, psychological, and sexual abuse by American soldiers.

American Psychological Association (APA): the scientific and professional organization that represents psychologists in the United States—the largest professional research psychology organization in America.

Amnesty International: a non-governmental organization originally founded in the 1960s to secure the human rights of political prisoners, now active in the field of human rights more generally.

Association for Psychological Science (APS): an international nonprofit organization (previously known as the American Psychological Society) concerned with the ethics, interests, and promotion of research in the field of psychology.

Authoritarian: a personality trait that is associated with both high levels of obedience and submission to authorities, as well as with support for the oppression of subordinates.

Banality of evil: a phrase that author Hannah Arendt coined to describe the Nazi war criminal Adolf Eichmann, who claimed he'd simply been "doing his job" while overseeing the slaughter of Jews during World War II. The term later came to refer to an idea that evil is commonplace and can be perpetrated by ordinary people.

BBC Prison Study: an empirical study conducted by social psychologists Stephen Reicher and S. Alexander Haslam and designed as a comparison and contrast to the Stanford Prison Experiment. It was broadcast as a television documentary in 2002 on the British Broadcasting Corporation (BBC).

Behaviorism: a major theory of learning that dominated psychology throughout the twentieth century, particularly in the middle of the century. Those scholars who supported the theory tended to view cognitive factors (that is, thinking) as less relevant than behaviors and preferred to study observable behaviors.

British Broadcasting Corporation (BBC): a British television and media broadcaster.

Catholic priest sexual-abuse cases: a series of allegations and convictions, most commonly in the late twentieth and early twenty-first century, of child sexual abuse committed by members of Catholic Church's clergy.

Cognitions: all mental abilities and processes associated with knowledge. The term includes memory, attention, problem solving, learning, and others.

Cognitive revolution: a broad movement beginning in the 1950s in several fields, such as psychology, anthropology, and linguistics. This movement focused on studying the internal thoughts, attitudes, motivations, and values that humans use to make sense of and interact with the world.

Conformity: a practice whereby individuals match their cognitions and behaviors to that of a group typically due to group norms and other social pressures.

Court-martial: a military court that typically determines the guilt and sentencing of military members.

Debriefed: a post-study intervention in research involving human subjects that provides participants with additional information about the study and probes them for psychological strain resulting from it.

Dehumanization: the act of overlooking or devaluing the human attributes of another person, typically viewing or treating the dehumanized as more impersonal, unequal, or animal.

Deindividuation: in social psychology, the loss of one's self-awareness and many of one's tendencies due to inclusion in a group or because one is anonymous.

Demand characteristics: a case where participants in a research study uncover the purpose of the study, which then influences their attitudes or behavior.

Disposition: in the field of psychology, an individual's internal characteristics, such as personality traits.

Egalitarian: a social doctrine that advocates treating people equally.

Enron fraud case: a case that occurred in 2001, when it emerged that Enron Corporation, a giant American energy company, was committing widespread institutionalized corruption and accounting fraud. This scandal resulted in the company's bankruptcy and the jailing of some executives.

Ghetto: an often poor, segregated section of a city that houses minority groups who generally have few other housing options.

Great Depression: the most significant economic recession in American history, beginning in 1929 and lasting through much of the 1930s.

Heroic Imagination Project: a nonprofit organization that Philip Zimbardo founded to research, teach, and promote heroism.

Human Subjects Research Review Board/Institutional review boards (IRBs): groups that review, monitor, and approve studies involving human participation. They were created in response to the many studies in the early to mid-twentieth century that used undisclosed deception and other means now considered unethical in the treatment of human subjects.

Individualism: a mindset whereby people think of themselves as individuals more than they think of themselves as members of a group.

Interactionist: in social and personality psychology, a common view that behavior is largely determined by the interaction of dispositional and situational factors.

Iraq War: a protracted conflict that began with the American-led invasion of Iraq in 2003.

Lucifer: in Christian tradition, a fallen angel who became the embodiment of evil.

Mass incarceration: the imprisonment of people at relatively high rates.

Need to belong: in psychology, the idea that humans have a fundamental need to feel included and accepted into groups and social circles.

Norms: in psychology, the accepted standards, values, and expected ways to behave and think in any given group (from a small group to a wider society or population). Each group defines its own norms, and a norm for one group may be unacceptable for another.

Obedience to authority: the deference and submission shown to authorities. Work by psychologist Stanley Milgram suggested that obedience to authority has a surprisingly strong influence on many people's behaviors.

Obedience studies: research that Stanley Milgram conducted at Yale University in the early 1960s in which he instructed volunteers to give electric shocks to a stranger, allegedly for an experiment on learning. Unaware the shocks were not real, most participants administered increasingly powerful shocks, despite their own fear and distress at doing so. This controversial experiment revealed the power that authority figures can have over people's behaviors.

Peer pressure: the social influence of a group to encourage attitude and behavioral change in peers and other group members.

Personality psychology: a field of psychology interested in how people differ on meaningful psychological variables.

Person–situation debate: a controversy found throughout the history of personality psychology concerned with determining the influence of personality/dispositional factors versus situational factors on behavior.

Political scientist: a person engaged in the systematic study of human political behavior and structures (such as the institutions of government, the ways in which political choices are made, international relations, and so on).

Positive psychology: a branch of psychology that focuses on the development of achievement rather than the treatment of pathology.

Power of the situation: the idea that situations have the potential to drastically influence human behavior.

Robber's Cave Experiment: A 1954 psychology study designed by the social psychologist Muzafer Sherif. He randomly split young boys at a summer camp in Oklahoma into two groups that competed over camp resources, leading to prejudice, negative stereotyping, and group conflict.

Rwanda genocides: the 1994 mass slaughter of up to one million people in Rwanda. Most victims were from the country's Tutsi ethnic minority group, killed by the Hutu majority.

Sadism/sadistic: deliberate cruelty or deriving pleasure from abusing others.

Schlesinger report: an independent investigation into the Abu Ghraib prison-abuse reports led by James Schlesinger in 2004.

Situation: the aspects of a context that are external to the person, serving as a focal point of analysis to create evil. The situation may mean anything from the surrounding environment, including other people, the weather, external rules and laws, and so on.

Situationists: people who typically believe that the power of situations significantly determines the behavior of the individuals in those situations, and who generally prefer situational explanations for behavior over those involving personality traits.

Situational forces: the powerful psychological pressures that the situation around a person places on him or her, whether he or she is aware of those pressures or not.

Sociologist: someone who studies the history, nature, formation, and structures of human societies.

Social psychology: a field of psychology interested in how situations influence people's thoughts, emotions, and behaviors.

Solitary confinement: a form of imprisonment that involves secluding a prisoner in a cell and preventing him or her from having any human contact, even with other prisoners.

Stanford Prison Experiment: a 1971 psychology study that Philip Zimbardo conducted at Stanford University in which he randomly assigned 12 volunteer participants to the role of either prisoner or guard in a makeshift prison. The experiment, intended to last two weeks, had to be ended early due to the guards' abuse of the prisoners whom they controlled.

Systemic factors: the influence of large-scale organizations or systems such as governments, cultures, and economies.

Trait: in personality psychology, a disposition or somewhat consistent pattern of behavior or cognition.

US Department of Defense (DoD): a branch of the US government charged with national security and the armed forces.

Vietnam War: an armed conflict from 1955 to 1975 between communist North Vietnam and South Vietnam, who were supported by the US military after 1961. All sides, including American troops, committed atrocities.

World War II: a global conflict that took place from 1939 to 1945 between the Axis Powers (Germany, Italy, and Japan) and the Allies (Great Britain, the Soviet Union, the United States, and other nations).

PEOPLE MENTIONED IN THE TEXT

Solomon Asch (1907–96) was a Polish social psychologist and professor emeritus at the University of Pennsylvania best known for his work on conformity.

Ali Banuazizi, is an Iranian American political scientist and professor at Boston College known for his work on the political cultures of the Middle East.

Ludy T. Benjamin Jr. (b. 1945) is an American psychologist and professor at Texas A&M University. His works have documented psychology's transformation into a science.

George W. Bush (b. 1946) was the 43rd President of the United States. A Republican, he served between 2001 and 2009.

Thomas Carnahan is an American organizational psychologist and formerly a professor at the University of Memphis. He is known for his work reexamining the Stanford Prison Experiment.

Dick Cheney (b. 1941) was the 46th Vice President of the United States. A Republican, he served from 2001 to 2009 under President George W. Bush.

Susan T. Fiske (b. 1952) is an American social psychologist and professor at Princeton University known for her work on social cognition and on prejudice and stereotyping.

Zeno Franco is an American clinical psychology professor at the Medical College of Wisconsin. His works have researched and defined heroism.

Ivan Frederick (b. 1966) is a former staff sergeant in the US Army. In 2004, he was convicted of war crimes for his mistreatment of detainees at Abu Ghraib prison in Iraq the previous year. After admitting to multiple charges including conspiracy, maltreatment of detainees, assault and indecent acts, he was sentenced to eight years in prison and dishonorably discharged.

Craig Haney is an American social psychologist and professor at the University of California at Santa Cruz known for his work on the psychological effects of incarceration and the effectiveness of prisons.

S. Alexander Haslam (b. 1962) is an Australian social psychologist and professor at the University of Queensland. His works examine conformity and tyranny, and question interpretations of the Stanford Prison Experiment and Stanley Milgram's obedience studies.

Robert Levine is an American social psychologist and professor at California State University at Fresno known for his work on the use and perception of time by people in different cultures.

George R. Mastroianni is an American psychologist and professor at the US Air Force Academy. His works apply psychological research to military training and practice.

Rose McDermott is an American political scientist and professor of international relations at Brown University known for her work on the predictors of political behavior.

Sam McFarland is an American social psychologist and professor emeritus at Western Kentucky University who focuses on human rights.

Stanley Milgram (1933–84) was an American social psychologist and professor at Yale University. His famous obedience studies demonstrated the extent to which people will conform to and obey authorities.

Walter Mischel (b. 1930) is an American psychologist and professor at Columbia University who has studied self-control, and developed an interactionist perspective to personality.

Siamak Movahedi is an Iranian American sociologist and professor of sociology at the University of Massachusetts. His research includes the study of the relationships between social structure and psychopathology.

Stephen Reicher is a British social psychologist and professor at the University of St. Andrews. He has studied human behavior in groups and conducted research on leaders and tyranny.

Donald Rumsfeld (b. 1932) was the 13th United States Secretary of Defense, from 1975 to 1977. He returned to serve as the 21st Secretary of Defense, from 2001 to 2006.

Carolyn Sherif (1922–82) was an American social psychologist who spent most of her career at Pennsylvania State University. She studied group conflict and cooperation.

Muzafer Sherif (1906–88) was a Turkish-American social psychologist. His key works were on social norms and the social conflict that results from the competition for resources. He designed the Robber's Cave Experiment.

Joan E. Sieber is an American psychologist and a professor emerita at California State University known for her work on scientific and research ethics.

Jeffry A. Simpson is an American social psychologist and professor at the University of Minnesota known for his work examining people's close relationships.

Martin B. Tolich is a New Zealand sociologist and professor at the University of Otago, New Zealand. His works include studies of research ethics.

WORKS CITED

WORKS CITED

Asch, Solomon E. "Studies of Independence and Conformity: I. A Minority of One Against a Unanimous Majority." *Psychological Monographs: General and Applied* 70, no. 9 (1956): 1–70.

Banuazizi, Ali and Siamak Movahedi, "Interpersonal Dynamics in a Simulated Prison: A Methodological Analysis." *American Psychologist* 30, no. 2 (1975): 152–60.

Carnahan, Thomas and Sam McFarland. "Revisiting the Stanford Prison Experiment: Could Participant Self-Selection Have Led to the Cruelty?" *Personality and Social Psychology Bulletin* 33, no. 5 (2007): 603–14.

Cushman, Jr., John H. "Outside Panel Faults Leaders of Pentagon for Prisoner Abuse." *New York Times*. August 24, 2004. Accessed September 17, 2015, http://www.nytimes.com/2004/08/24/politics/24CND-ABUS.html.

Donnellan, M. Brent, et al. "Not So Situational," *Observer*. June/July 2007. Accessed September 27, 2015. http://www.psychologicalscience.org/index.php/publications/observer/2007/june-july-07/not-so-situational.html.

Drury, Scott, Scott A. Hutchens, Duane E. Shuttlesworth, and Carole L. White. "Philip G. Zimbardo on His Career and the Stanford Prison Experiment's 40th Anniversary." *History of Psychology* 15, no. 2 (2012): 161–70.

Fiske, Susan T., L. T. Harris, and A. J. Cuddy. "Social Psychology. Why Ordinary People Torture Enemy Prisoners." *Science* 306, no. 5701 (2004): 1482–3.

Franco, Zeno and Philip Zimbardo, "The Banality of Heroism." *Greater Good Science Center*. September 1, 2006. Accessed September 27, 2015. http://greatergood.berkeley.edu/article/item/the_banality_of_heroism.

Haney, Craig. *Reforming Punishment: Psychological Limits to the Pains of Imprisonment*. Washington DC: American Psychological Association, 2006.

"A Culture of Harm Taming the Dynamics of Cruelty in Supermax Prisons." *Criminal Justice and Behavior* 35, no. 8 (2008): 956–84.

"Counting Casualties in the War on Prisoners." *USFL Rev.* 43 (2008): 87–138.

Haney, Craig, Curtis Banks, and Philip Zimbardo, "Interpersonal Dynamics in a Simulated Prison." *International Journal of Criminology and Penology*, 1, (1973): 69–97.

Haney, Craig and Philip Zimbardo. "The Past and Future of US Prison Policy: Twenty-five Years after the Stanford Prison Experiment." *American Psychologist* 53, no. 7 (1998): 709–27.

Haslam, S. Alexander and Stephen D. Reicher. "Contesting the 'Nature' Of Conformity: What Milgram and Zimbardo's Studies Really Show." *PLoS Biology* 10, no. 11 (2012): e1001426.

Herbert, Wray. "The Banality of Evil," *Observer*. April 2007. Accessed September 27, 2015. http://aps.psychologicalscience.org/index.php/publications/observer/2007/april-07/the-banality-of-evil.html.

Krakovsky, Marina. "Zimbardo Unbound." *Stanford Magazine*. May/June 2007. Accessed September 27, 2015. https://alumni.stanford.edu/get/page/magazine/article/?article_id=32541.

Levine, Robert. "The Evil That Men Do." *American Scientist*. September-October 2007. Accessed September 15, 2015, http://www.americanscientist.org/bookshelf/content2/2007/5/the-evil-that-men-do.

Maslach, Christina. "Emperor of the Edge." *Psychology Today*. September 1, 2000. Accessed September 15, 2015, https://www.psychologytoday.com/articles/200009/emperor-the-edge.

Mastroianni, George R. "Zimbardo's Apple." *Analyses of Social Issues and Public Policy* 7, no. 1 (2007): 251–254.

McDermott, Rose. "Reviewed Work: *The Lucifer Effect: Understanding How Good People Turn Evil* by Philip Zimbardo." *Political Psychology* 28, No. 5 (2007): 644–6.

Moorehead-Slaughter, Olivia. "Ethics and National Security," *Monitor on Psychology*. April 2006. Accessed September 17, 2015, http:// www.apa.org/monitor/apr06/security.aspx.

Mischel, Walter. "Toward a Cognitive Social Learning Reconceptualization of Personality." *Psychological Review* 80, no. 4 (1973): 252–83.

Reicher, Stephen and S. Alexander Haslam. "Rethinking the Psychology of Tyranny: The BBC Prison Study." *British Journal of Social Psychology* 45, no. 1 (2006): 1–40.

Sieber, Joan E. and Martin B. Tolich. *Planning Ethically Responsible Research*. Thousand Oaks: Sage Publications, 2012.

Slavich, George M. "On 50 Years of Giving Psychology Away: An Interview with Philip Zimbardo." *Teaching of Psychology* 36, no. 4 (2009): 278–84.

Zimbardo, Philip G. "On the Ethics of Intervention in Human Psychological Research: With Special Reference to the Stanford Prison Experiment." *Cognition* 2, no. 2 (1973): 243–56.

"Recollections of a Social Psychologist's Career: An Interview with Dr. Philip Zimbardo." *Journal of Social Behavior and Personality* 14, No. 1 (1999): 1–22.

"Power turns good soldiers into 'bad apples.'" *The Boston Globe*. May 9, 2004. Accessed September 16, 2015, http://www.boston.com/news/globe/editorial_opinion/oped/articles/2004/05/09/power_turns_good_soldiers_into_bad_apples/.

The Lucifer Effect: Understanding How Good People Turn Evil. New York: Random House, 2007.

"Person X Situation X System Dynamics." *The Lucifer Effect*. Accessed September 27, 2015. http://www.lucifereffect.com/apsrejoinder.htm.

"What Makes a Hero?" *Greater Good Science Center*. January 18, 2011. Accessed September 27, 2015. http://greatergood.berkeley.edu/article/item/what_makes_a_hero/.

Zimbardo, Philip G. and John N. Boyd. "Putting Time in Perspective: A Valid, Reliable Individual-Differences Metric." *Journal of Personality and Social Psychology* 77, no. 6 (1999): 1271–88.

Zimbardo, Philip G., Christina Maslach, and Craig Haney. "Reflections on the Stanford Prison Experiment: Genesis, Transformations, Consequences." Obedience to authority: Current perspectives on the Milgram paradigm (2000): 193–237.

THE MACAT LIBRARY
BY DISCIPLINE

AFRICANA STUDIES

Chinua Achebe's *An Image of Africa: Racism in Conrad's Heart of Darkness*
W. E. B. Du Bois's *The Souls of Black Folk*
Zora Neale Huston's *Characteristics of Negro Expression*
Martin Luther King Jr's *Why We Can't Wait*
Toni Morrison's *Playing in the Dark: Whiteness in the American Literary Imagination*

ANTHROPOLOGY

Arjun Appadurai's *Modernity at Large: Cultural Dimensions of Globalisation*
Philippe Ariès's *Centuries of Childhood*
Franz Boas's *Race, Language and Culture*
Kim Chan & Renée Mauborgne's *Blue Ocean Strategy*
Jared Diamond's *Guns, Germs & Steel: the Fate of Human Societies*
Jared Diamond's *Collapse: How Societies Choose to Fail or Survive*
E. E. Evans-Pritchard's *Witchcraft, Oracles and Magic Among the Azande*
James Ferguson's *The Anti-Politics Machine*
Clifford Geertz's *The Interpretation of Cultures*
David Graeber's *Debt: the First 5000 Years*
Karen Ho's *Liquidated: An Ethnography of Wall Street*
Geert Hofstede's *Culture's Consequences: Comparing Values, Behaviors, Institutes and Organizations across Nations*
Claude Lévi-Strauss's *Structural Anthropology*
Jay Macleod's *Ain't No Makin' It: Aspirations and Attainment in a Low-Income Neighborhood*
Saba Mahmood's *The Politics of Piety: The Islamic Revival and the Feminist Subjec*t
Marcel Mauss's *The Gift*

BUSINESS

Jean Lave & Etienne Wenger's *Situated Learning*
Theodore Levitt's *Marketing Myopia*
Burton G. Malkiel's *A Random Walk Down Wall Street*
Douglas McGregor's *The Human Side of Enterprise*
Michael Porter's *Competitive Strategy: Creating and Sustaining Superior Performance*
John Kotter's *Leading Change*
C. K. Prahalad & Gary Hamel's *The Core Competence of the Corporation*

CRIMINOLOGY

Michelle Alexander's *The New Jim Crow: Mass Incarceration in the Age of Colorblindness*
Michael R. Gottfredson & Travis Hirschi's *A General Theory of Crime*
Richard Herrnstein & Charles A. Murray's *The Bell Curve: Intelligence and Class Structure in American Life*
Elizabeth Loftus's *Eyewitness Testimony*
Jay Macleod's *Ain't No Makin' It: Aspirations and Attainment in a Low-Income Neighborhood*
Philip Zimbardo's *The Lucifer Effect*

ECONOMICS

Janet Abu-Lughod's *Before European Hegemony*
Ha-Joon Chang's *Kicking Away the Ladder*
David Brion Davis's *The Problem of Slavery in the Age of Revolution*
Milton Friedman's *The Role of Monetary Policy*
Milton Friedman's *Capitalism and Freedom*
David Graeber's *Debt: the First 5000 Years*
Friedrich Hayek's *The Road to Serfdom*
Karen Ho's *Liquidated: An Ethnography of Wall Street*

John Maynard Keynes's *The General Theory of Employment, Interest and Money*
Charles P. Kindleberger's *Manias, Panics and Crashes*
Robert Lucas's *Why Doesn't Capital Flow from Rich to Poor Countries?*
Burton G. Malkiel's *A Random Walk Down Wall Street*
Thomas Robert Malthus's *An Essay on the Principle of Population*
Karl Marx's *Capital*
Thomas Piketty's *Capital in the Twenty-First Century*
Amartya Sen's *Development as Freedom*
Adam Smith's *The Wealth of Nations*
Nassim Nicholas Taleb's *The Black Swan: The Impact of the Highly Improbable*
Amos Tversky's & Daniel Kahneman's *Judgment under Uncertainty: Heuristics and Biases*
Mahbub Ul Haq's *Reflections on Human Development*
Max Weber's *The Protestant Ethic and the Spirit of Capitalism*

FEMINISM AND GENDER STUDIES

Judith Butler's *Gender Trouble*
Simone De Beauvoir's *The Second Sex*
Michel Foucault's *History of Sexuality*
Betty Friedan's *The Feminine Mystique*
Saba Mahmood's *The Politics of Piety: The Islamic Revival and the Feminist Subject*
Joan Wallach Scott's *Gender and the Politics of History*
Mary Wollstonecraft's *A Vindication of the Rights of Woman*
Virginia Woolf's *A Room of One's Own*

GEOGRAPHY

The Brundtland Report's *Our Common Future*
Rachel Carson's *Silent Spring*
Charles Darwin's *On the Origin of Species*
James Ferguson's *The Anti-Politics Machine*
Jane Jacobs's *The Death and Life of Great American Cities*
James Lovelock's *Gaia: A New Look at Life on Earth*
Amartya Sen's *Development as Freedom*
Mathis Wackernagel & William Rees's *Our Ecological Footprint*

HISTORY

Janet Abu-Lughod's *Before European Hegemony*
Benedict Anderson's *Imagined Communities*
Bernard Bailyn's *The Ideological Origins of the American Revolution*
Hanna Batatu's *The Old Social Classes And The Revolutionary Movements Of Iraq*
Christopher Browning's *Ordinary Men: Reserve Police Batallion 101 and the Final Solution in Poland*
Edmund Burke's *Reflections on the Revolution in France*
William Cronon's *Nature's Metropolis: Chicago And The Great West*
Alfred W. Crosby's *The Columbian Exchange*
Hamid Dabashi's *Iran: A People Interrupted*
David Brion Davis's *The Problem of Slavery in the Age of Revolution*
Nathalie Zemon Davis's *The Return of Martin Guerre*
Jared Diamond's *Guns, Germs & Steel: the Fate of Human Societies*
Frank Dikotter's *Mao's Great Famine*
John W Dower's *War Without Mercy: Race And Power In The Pacific War*
W. E. B. Du Bois's *The Souls of Black Folk*
Richard J. Evans's *In Defence of History*
Lucien Febvre's *The Problem of Unbelief in the 16th Century*
Sheila Fitzpatrick's *Everyday Stalinism*

Eric Foner's *Reconstruction: America's Unfinished Revolution, 1863-1877*
Michel Foucault's *Discipline and Punish*
Michel Foucault's *History of Sexuality*
Francis Fukuyama's *The End of History and the Last Man*
John Lewis Gaddis's *We Now Know: Rethinking Cold War History*
Ernest Gellner's *Nations and Nationalism*
Eugene Genovese's *Roll, Jordan, Roll: The World the Slaves Made*
Carlo Ginzburg's *The Night Battles*
Daniel Goldhagen's *Hitler's Willing Executioners*
Jack Goldstone's *Revolution and Rebellion in the Early Modern World*
Antonio Gramsci's *The Prison Notebooks*
Alexander Hamilton, John Jay & James Madison's *The Federalist Papers*
Christopher Hill's *The World Turned Upside Down*
Carole Hillenbrand's *The Crusades: Islamic Perspectives*
Thomas Hobbes's *Leviathan*
Eric Hobsbawm's *The Age Of Revolution*
John A. Hobson's *Imperialism: A Study*
Albert Hourani's *History of the Arab Peoples*
Samuel P. Huntington's *The Clash of Civilizations and the Remaking of World Order*
C. L. R. James's *The Black Jacobins*
Tony Judt's *Postwar: A History of Europe Since 1945*
Ernst Kantorowicz's *The King's Two Bodies: A Study in Medieval Political Theology*
Paul Kennedy's *The Rise and Fall of the Great Powers*
Ian Kershaw's *The "Hitler Myth": Image and Reality in the Third Reich*
John Maynard Keynes's *The General Theory of Employment, Interest and Money*
Charles P. Kindleberger's *Manias, Panics and Crashes*
Martin Luther King Jr's *Why We Can't Wait*
Henry Kissinger's *World Order: Reflections on the Character of Nations and the Course of History*
Thomas Kuhn's *The Structure of Scientific Revolutions*
Georges Lefebvre's *The Coming of the French Revolution*
John Locke's *Two Treatises of Government*
Niccolò Machiavelli's *The Prince*
Thomas Robert Malthus's *An Essay on the Principle of Population*
Mahmood Mamdani's *Citizen and Subject: Contemporary Africa And The Legacy Of Late Colonialism*
Karl Marx's *Capital*
Stanley Milgram's *Obedience to Authority*
John Stuart Mill's *On Liberty*
Thomas Paine's *Common Sense*
Thomas Paine's *Rights of Man*
Geoffrey Parker's *Global Crisis: War, Climate Change and Catastrophe in the Seventeenth Century*
Jonathan Riley-Smith's *The First Crusade and the Idea of Crusading*
Jean-Jacques Rousseau's *The Social Contract*
Joan Wallach Scott's *Gender and the Politics of History*
Theda Skocpol's *States and Social Revolutions*
Adam Smith's *The Wealth of Nations*
Timothy Snyder's *Bloodlands: Europe Between Hitler and Stalin*
Sun Tzu's *The Art of War*
Keith Thomas's *Religion and the Decline of Magic*
Thucydides's *The History of the Peloponnesian War*
Frederick Jackson Turner's *The Significance of the Frontier in American History*
Odd Arne Westad's *The Global Cold War: Third World Interventions And The Making Of Our Times*

The Macat Library By Discipline

LITERATURE

Chinua Achebe's *An Image of Africa: Racism in Conrad's Heart of Darkness*
Roland Barthes's *Mythologies*
Homi K. Bhabha's *The Location of Culture*
Judith Butler's *Gender Trouble*
Simone De Beauvoir's *The Second Sex*
Ferdinand De Saussure's *Course in General Linguistics*
T. S. Eliot's *The Sacred Wood: Essays on Poetry and Criticism*
Zora Neale Huston's *Characteristics of Negro Expression*
Toni Morrison's *Playing in the Dark: Whiteness in the American Literary Imagination*
Edward Said's *Orientalism*
Gayatri Chakravorty Spivak's *Can the Subaltern Speak?*
Mary Wollstonecraft's *A Vindication of the Rights of Women*
Virginia Woolf's *A Room of One's Own*

PHILOSOPHY

Elizabeth Anscombe's *Modern Moral Philosophy*
Hannah Arendt's *The Human Condition*
Aristotle's *Metaphysics*
Aristotle's *Nicomachean Ethics*
Edmund Gettier's *Is Justified True Belief Knowledge?*
Georg Wilhelm Friedrich Hegel's *Phenomenology of Spirit*
David Hume's *Dialogues Concerning Natural Religion*
David Hume's *The Enquiry for Human Understanding*
Immanuel Kant's *Religion within the Boundaries of Mere Reason*
Immanuel Kant's *Critique of Pure Reason*
Søren Kierkegaard's *The Sickness Unto Death*
Søren Kierkegaard's *Fear and Trembling*
C. S. Lewis's *The Abolition of Man*
Alasdair MacIntyre's *After Virtue*
Marcus Aurelius's *Meditations*
Friedrich Nietzsche's *On the Genealogy of Morality*
Friedrich Nietzsche's *Beyond Good and Evil*
Plato's *Republic*
Plato's *Symposium*
Jean-Jacques Rousseau's *The Social Contract*
Gilbert Ryle's *The Concept of Mind*
Baruch Spinoza's *Ethics*
Sun Tzu's *The Art of War*
Ludwig Wittgenstein's *Philosophical Investigations*

POLITICS

Benedict Anderson's *Imagined Communities*
Aristotle's *Politics*
Bernard Bailyn's *The Ideological Origins of the American Revolution*
Edmund Burke's *Reflections on the Revolution in France*
John C. Calhoun's *A Disquisition on Government*
Ha-Joon Chang's *Kicking Away the Ladder*
Hamid Dabashi's *Iran: A People Interrupted*
Hamid Dabashi's *Theology of Discontent: The Ideological Foundation of the Islamic Revolution in Iran*
Robert Dahl's *Democracy and its Critics*
Robert Dahl's *Who Governs?*
David Brion Davis's *The Problem of Slavery in the Age of Revolution*

Alexis De Tocqueville's *Democracy in America*
James Ferguson's *The Anti-Politics Machine*
Frank Dikotter's *Mao's Great Famine*
Sheila Fitzpatrick's *Everyday Stalinism*
Eric Foner's *Reconstruction: America's Unfinished Revolution, 1863-1877*
Milton Friedman's *Capitalism and Freedom*
Francis Fukuyama's *The End of History and the Last Man*
John Lewis Gaddis's *We Now Know: Rethinking Cold War History*
Ernest Gellner's *Nations and Nationalism*
David Graeber's *Debt: the First 5000 Years*
Antonio Gramsci's *The Prison Notebooks*
Alexander Hamilton, John Jay & James Madison's *The Federalist Papers*
Friedrich Hayek's *The Road to Serfdom*
Christopher Hill's *The World Turned Upside Down*
Thomas Hobbes's *Leviathan*
John A. Hobson's *Imperialism: A Study*
Samuel P. Huntington's *The Clash of Civilizations and the Remaking of World Order*
Tony Judt's *Postwar: A History of Europe Since 1945*
David C. Kang's *China Rising: Peace, Power and Order in East Asia*
Paul Kennedy's *The Rise and Fall of Great Powers*
Robert Keohane's *After Hegemony*
Martin Luther King Jr.'s *Why We Can't Wait*
Henry Kissinger's *World Order: Reflections on the Character of Nations and the Course of History*
John Locke's *Two Treatises of Government*
Niccolò Machiavelli's *The Prince*
Thomas Robert Malthus's *An Essay on the Principle of Population*
Mahmood Mamdani's *Citizen and Subject: Contemporary Africa And The Legacy Of Late Colonialism*
Karl Marx's *Capital*
John Stuart Mill's *On Liberty*
John Stuart Mill's *Utilitarianism*
Hans Morgenthau's *Politics Among Nations*
Thomas Paine's *Common Sense*
Thomas Paine's *Rights of Man*
Thomas Piketty's *Capital in the Twenty-First Century*
Robert D. Putman's *Bowling Alone*
John Rawls's *Theory of Justice*
Jean-Jacques Rousseau's *The Social Contract*
Theda Skocpol's *States and Social Revolutions*
Adam Smith's *The Wealth of Nations*
Sun Tzu's *The Art of War*
Henry David Thoreau's *Civil Disobedience*
Thucydides's *The History of the Peloponnesian War*
Kenneth Waltz's *Theory of International Politics*
Max Weber's *Politics as a Vocation*
Odd Arne Westad's *The Global Cold War: Third World Interventions And The Making Of Our Times*

POSTCOLONIAL STUDIES

Roland Barthes's *Mythologies*
Frantz Fanon's *Black Skin, White Masks*
Homi K. Bhabha's *The Location of Culture*
Gustavo Gutiérrez's *A Theology of Liberation*
Edward Said's *Orientalism*
Gayatri Chakravorty Spivak's *Can the Subaltern Speak?*

The Macat Library By Discipline

PSYCHOLOGY

Gordon Allport's *The Nature of Prejudice*
Alan Baddeley & Graham Hitch's *Aggression: A Social Learning Analysis*
Albert Bandura's *Aggression: A Social Learning Analysis*
Leon Festinger's *A Theory of Cognitive Dissonance*
Sigmund Freud's *The Interpretation of Dreams*
Betty Friedan's *The Feminine Mystique*
Michael R. Gottfredson & Travis Hirschi's *A General Theory of Crime*
Eric Hoffer's *The True Believer: Thoughts on the Nature of Mass Movements*
William James's *Principles of Psychology*
Elizabeth Loftus's *Eyewitness Testimony*
A. H. Maslow's *A Theory of Human Motivation*
Stanley Milgram's *Obedience to Authority*
Steven Pinker's *The Better Angels of Our Nature*
Oliver Sacks's *The Man Who Mistook His Wife For a Hat*
Richard Thaler & Cass Sunstein's *Nudge: Improving Decisions About Health, Wealth and Happiness*
Amos Tversky's *Judgment under Uncertainty: Heuristics and Biases*
Philip Zimbardo's *The Lucifer Effect*

SCIENCE

Rachel Carson's *Silent Spring*
William Cronon's *Nature's Metropolis: Chicago And The Great West*
Alfred W. Crosby's *The Columbian Exchange*
Charles Darwin's *On the Origin of Species*
Richard Dawkin's *The Selfish Gene*
Thomas Kuhn's *The Structure of Scientific Revolutions*
Geoffrey Parker's *Global Crisis: War, Climate Change and Catastrophe in the Seventeenth Century*
Mathis Wackernagel & William Rees's *Our Ecological Footprint*

SOCIOLOGY

Michelle Alexander's *The New Jim Crow: Mass Incarceration in the Age of Colorblindness*
Gordon Allport's *The Nature of Prejudice*
Albert Bandura's *Aggression: A Social Learning Analysis*
Hanna Batatu's *The Old Social Classes And The Revolutionary Movements Of Iraq*
Ha-Joon Chang's *Kicking Away the Ladder*
W. E. B. Du Bois's *The Souls of Black Folk*
Émile Durkheim's *On Suicide*
Frantz Fanon's *Black Skin, White Masks*
Frantz Fanon's *The Wretched of the Earth*
Eric Foner's *Reconstruction: America's Unfinished Revolution, 1863-1877*
Eugene Genovese's *Roll, Jordan, Roll: The World the Slaves Made*
Jack Goldstone's *Revolution and Rebellion in the Early Modern World*
Antonio Gramsci's *The Prison Notebooks*
Richard Herrnstein & Charles A Murray's *The Bell Curve: Intelligence and Class Structure in American Life*
Eric Hoffer's *The True Believer: Thoughts on the Nature of Mass Movements*
Jane Jacobs's *The Death and Life of Great American Cities*
Robert Lucas's *Why Doesn't Capital Flow from Rich to Poor Countries?*
Jay Macleod's *Ain't No Makin' It: Aspirations and Attainment in a Low Income Neighborhood*
Elaine May's *Homeward Bound: American Families in the Cold War Era*
Douglas McGregor's *The Human Side of Enterprise*
C. Wright Mills's *The Sociological Imagination*

Thomas Piketty's *Capital in the Twenty-First Century*
Robert D. Putman's *Bowling Alone*
David Riesman's *The Lonely Crowd: A Study of the Changing American Character*
Edward Said's *Orientalism*
Joan Wallach Scott's *Gender and the Politics of History*
Theda Skocpol's *States and Social Revolutions*
Max Weber's *The Protestant Ethic and the Spirit of Capitalism*

THEOLOGY

Augustine's *Confessions*
Benedict's *Rule of St Benedict*
Gustavo Gutiérrez's *A Theology of Liberation*
Carole Hillenbrand's *The Crusades: Islamic Perspectives*
David Hume's *Dialogues Concerning Natural Religion*
Immanuel Kant's *Religion within the Boundaries of Mere Reason*
Ernst Kantorowicz's *The King's Two Bodies: A Study in Medieval Political Theology*
Søren Kierkegaard's *The Sickness Unto Death*
C. S. Lewis's *The Abolition of Man*
Saba Mahmood's *The Politics of Piety: The Islamic Revival and the Feminist Subject*
Baruch Spinoza's *Ethics*
Keith Thomas's *Religion and the Decline of Magic*

COMING SOON

Chris Argyris's *The Individual and the Organisation*
Seyla Benhabib's *The Rights of Others*
Walter Benjamin's *The Work Of Art in the Age of Mechanical Reproduction*
John Berger's *Ways of Seeing*
Pierre Bourdieu's *Outline of a Theory of Practice*
Mary Douglas's *Purity and Danger*
Roland Dworkin's *Taking Rights Seriously*
James G. March's *Exploration and Exploitation in Organisational Learning*
Ikujiro Nonaka's *A Dynamic Theory of Organizational Knowledge Creation*
Griselda Pollock's *Vision and Difference*
Amartya Sen's *Inequality Re-Examined*
Susan Sontag's *On Photography*
Yasser Tabbaa's *The Transformation of Islamic Art*
Ludwig von Mises's *Theory of Money and Credit*

Macat Disciplines

Access the greatest ideas and thinkers across entire disciplines, including

AFRICANA STUDIES

Chinua Achebe's *An Image of Africa: Racism in Conrad's Heart of Darkness*

W. E. B. Du Bois's *The Souls of Black Folk*

Zora Neale Hurston's *Characteristics of Negro Expression*

Martin Luther King Jr.'s *Why We Can't Wait*

Toni Morrison's *Playing in the Dark: Whiteness in the American Literary Imagination*

Macat analyses are available from all good bookshops and libraries.

Access hundreds of analyses through one, multimedia tool.
Join free for one month **library.macat.com**

Macat Disciplines

Access the greatest ideas and thinkers across entire disciplines, including

FEMINISM, GENDER AND QUEER STUDIES

Simone De Beauvoir's
The Second Sex

Michel Foucault's
History of Sexuality

Betty Friedan's
The Feminine Mystique

Saba Mahmood's
The Politics of Piety: The Islamic Revival and the Feminist Subject

Joan Wallach Scott's
Gender and the Politics of History

Mary Wollstonecraft's
A Vindication of the Rights of Woman

Virginia Woolf's
A Room of One's Own

Judith Butler's
Gender Trouble

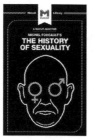

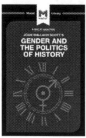

Macat analyses are available from all good bookshops and libraries.

Access hundreds of analyses through one, multimedia tool.

Join free for one month **library.macat.com**

Macat Disciplines

Access the greatest ideas and thinkers across entire disciplines, including

INEQUALITY

Ha-Joon Chang's, *Kicking Away the Ladder*

David Graeber's, *Debt: The First 5000 Years*

Robert E. Lucas's, *Why Doesn't Capital Flow from Rich To Poor Countries?*

Thomas Piketty's, *Capital in the Twenty-First Century*

Amartya Sen's, *Inequality Re-Examined*

Mahbub Ul Haq's, *Reflections on Human Development*

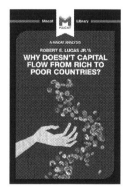

Macat analyses are available from all good bookshops and libraries.

Access hundreds of analyses through one, multimedia tool.
Join free for one month **library.macat.com**

Macat Disciplines

Access the greatest ideas and thinkers across entire disciplines, including

CRIMINOLOGY

Michelle Alexander's
The New Jim Crow: Mass Incarceration in the Age of Colorblindness

Michael R. Gottfredson & Travis Hirschi's
A General Theory of Crime

Elizabeth Loftus's
Eyewitness Testimony

Richard Herrnstein & Charles A. Murray's
The Bell Curve: Intelligence and Class Structure in American Life

Jay Macleod's
Ain't No Makin' It: Aspirations and Attainment in a Low-Income Neighborhood

Philip Zimbardo's
The Lucifer Effect

Macat analyses are available from all good bookshops and libraries.

Access hundreds of analyses through one, multimedia tool.
Join free for one month **library.macat.com**

Macat Disciplines

Access the greatest ideas and thinkers across entire disciplines, including

Postcolonial Studies

Roland Barthes's *Mythologies*
Frantz Fanon's *Black Skin, White Masks*
Homi K. Bhabha's *The Location of Culture*
Gustavo Gutiérrez's *A Theology of Liberation*
Edward Said's *Orientalism*
Gayatri Chakravorty Spivak's *Can the Subaltern Speak?*

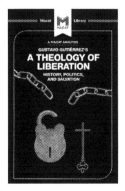
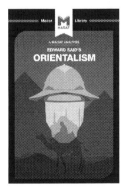

Macat analyses are available from all good bookshops and libraries.

Access hundreds of analyses through one, multimedia tool.
Join free for one month **library.macat.com**

Macat Disciplines

*Access the greatest ideas and thinkers
across entire disciplines, including*

GLOBALIZATION

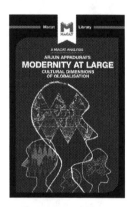

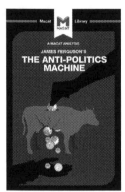

Arjun Appadurai's, *Modernity at Large:
Cultural Dimensions of Globalisation*

James Ferguson's, *The Anti-Politics Machine*

Geert Hofstede's, *Culture's Consequences*

Amartya Sen's, *Development as Freedom*

Macat analyses are available from all good bookshops and libraries.

Access hundreds of analyses through one, multimedia tool.
Join free for one month **library.macat.com**

Macat Pairs

Analyse historical and modern issues from opposite sides of an argument. Pairs include:

HOW TO RUN AN ECONOMY

John Maynard Keynes's
The General Theory OF Employment, Interest and Money

Classical economics suggests that market economies are self-correcting in times of recession or depression, and tend toward full employment and output. But English economist John Maynard Keynes disagrees.

In his ground-breaking 1936 study *The General Theory*, Keynes argues that traditional economics has misunderstood the causes of unemployment. Employment is not determined by the price of labor; it is directly linked to demand. Keynes believes market economies are by nature unstable, and so require government intervention. Spurred on by the social catastrophe of the Great Depression of the 1930s, he sets out to revolutionize the way the world thinks

Milton Friedman's
The Role of Monetary Policy

Friedman's 1968 paper changed the course of economic theory. In just 17 pages, he demolished existing theory and outlined an effective alternate monetary policy designed to secure 'high employment, stable prices and rapid growth.'

Friedman demonstrated that monetary policy plays a vital role in broader economic stability and argued that economists got their monetary policy wrong in the 1950s and 1960s by misunderstanding the relationship between inflation and unemployment. Previous generations of economists had believed that governments could permanently decrease unemployment by permitting inflation—and vice versa. Friedman's most original contribution was to show that this supposed trade-off is an illusion that only works in the short term.

Macat analyses are available from all good bookshops and libraries.

Access hundreds of analyses through one, multimedia tool.
Join free for one month **library.macat.com**

Macat Disciplines

Access the greatest ideas and thinkers across entire disciplines, including

THE FUTURE OF DEMOCRACY

Robert A. Dahl's, *Democracy and Its Critics*
Robert A. Dahl's, *Who Governs?*
Alexis De Toqueville's, *Democracy in America*
Niccolò Machiavelli's, *The Prince*
John Stuart Mill's, *On Liberty*
Robert D. Putnam's, *Bowling Alone*
Jean-Jacques Rousseau's, *The Social Contract*
Henry David Thoreau's, *Civil Disobedience*

Macat Disciplines

Access the greatest ideas and thinkers across entire disciplines, including

TOTALITARIANISM

Sheila Fitzpatrick's, *Everyday Stalinism*
Ian Kershaw's, *The "Hitler Myth"*
Timothy Snyder's, *Bloodlands*

Macat analyses are available from all good bookshops and libraries.

Access hundreds of analyses through one, multimedia tool.
Join free for one month **library.macat.com**

Printed in the United States
by Baker & Taylor Publisher Services